The United Pastors in Mission

Messages for Modern Times

Edited by

Dr. Larry L. Macon

KENDALL/HUNT PUBLISHING COMPANY
4050 Westmark Drive   Dubuque, Iowa 52002

Cover image courtesy of Corel.

Copyright © 1998 by Dr. Larry L. Macon

ISBN 0-7872-2410-3

Library of Congress Catalog Card Number: 98-66441

Printed in the United States of America
10 9 8 7 6 5 4 3 2 1

*To my wife, Marilyn Magwood Macon,
and my two sons, Larry Lawrence, Jr., and
Daniel Lawrence, and in dedication to the
memory of God's great servant,
Dr. Samuel D. Proctor.*

Contents

Preface

These messages come from the hearts, minds, and souls of the United Pastors in Mission, leading pastors and preachers in the Greater Cleveland, Ohio area. They are prophetic and endowed with a 21st-century flair. These are messages for this modern time. Crafted with the excellence of theological reflections and methodological principles of accuracy, they are modern in the sense that these preachers have transposed 1st- century texts for modern times.

When you read these sermons and messages you will be pulled by not only the art of preaching, but also by the deep conviction and drawing force of the Holy Spirit. These sermons are not only "preachable" but "livable." They are messages that will so bless your life, you are bound to change your perspective on the issue of sin not only to be saved but to serve. The heart of these pastors is buried in these sermons. One cannot read *Messages for Modern Times* without feeling the strong love and compassion, strengths and struggles, push and pull of these ministers as they pour out these exciting and sometimes challenging revelations. They are truly ahead of their time.

I am grateful for those pastors who serve under my leadership as president of the United Pastors in Mission. They have been great assets not only to the Greater Cleveland area, the State of Ohio, the nation, and the world, but more rightly, to the Kingdom of God. You will hear the Kingdom coming alive in these modern times.

The sermon I preached entitled, "It Is Finished," was presented at one of our city's annual Good Friday services. It was so well received by the listeners that I felt God led me to share it in this book. This sermon was inspired by God, which means it was "God-breathed" and needed to be read by modern folk.

I am grateful to my senior mentor and friend, Dr. Otis Moss, Jr., pastor of the Olivet Institutional Baptist Church in Cleveland. Dr. Moss was called to preach at the young age of five or six. He publicly acknowledged his calling at seventeen, and since then has traveled the nation and the world, speaking and preaching to presidents and other heads of state. He served as co-pastor of the Ebenezer Baptist Church in Atlanta, Georgia with the late Rev. Dr. Martin Luther King, Sr. Dr. Moss preached a most inspiring word at our

Good Friday Service entitled, "Father, Into Thy hands I Commend My Spirit."

The next message is by Dr. Marvin A. McMickle, who presents the weekly lecture at the United Pastors in Mission. He is a son of the ministry of Dr. William Augustus Jones, Jr., pastor of Bethany Baptist Church in Brooklyn, New York. Like the Rev. Dr. Gardner Taylor, Dr. McMickle is a "Dean of Preachers." Read his sermon carefully as he dissects the Word as skillfully as a master surgeon in his sermon entitled, "Testimony of the Tortured."

The Rev. Dr. Albert T. Rowan in "A Time to Talk" illustrates the kind of communication the people of God will need to use in the 21st Century. This is for him and for us a "God talk" that is truly open in the Kingdom of God.

Next, Dr. Sterling Glover of the historic Emmanuel Baptist Church is not only prophetic in "Liberation Thru the Cross," but also priestly in his execution of the message. To read this sermon is to come extremely close to the profound yet never to depart from that which is real.

Immediately following is the message by Rev. Rodney Maiden, a young evangelist within our community. He is our modern-day Paul in search of potential believers. To read and hear him is to be caught up by a message of such conviction that you find yourself in the position of the soldier in Acts during the imprisonment of Paul and Silas. You too will ask, "What must I do to be saved?"

The Rev. Richard E. Barnes brings to our book both style and character. His sermon, "The Road to Heaven," is persuasive and told with humor. The art of true preaching is one that can include what I call "tasteful" humor. Too often, I have heard "tasteless" humor expressed in a message. Walk with Rev. Barnes along the road of theological truths and excellent story-telling.

Rev. C. Jay Matthews furthers this journey of the Christian in his sermon, "The Problem of Serving Two Masters," by suggesting that economic empowerment occurs when one serves God.

Dr. Timothy James follows and asserts in his sermon, "The Truth is The Light," that one has to walk in the light of the Christ of God. Hear him as he lifts up the duality of light and darkness through the great theologian William Barclay.

"A Satanic Breakthrough" is indeed one of the finest messages for any Christian who experiences trials and tribulations like Job of the Bible. The author of this sermon, Larry Lawrence Harris, will show you how God will help you to overcome when Satan breaks through in your life.

Rev. Henry James Payden, Sr. is the "Prophet Amos" of our day. He has a way of pointing out the sin and ushering in the provider. Read carefully his sermon, "Standing on the Rock."

Last is a message by one of the greatest scholars of our day. Dr. William H. Myers of the Ashland Theological Seminary delivers a message entitled, "No Risks, No Rewards." You will be at risk as well as rewarded in reading this sermon. These are truly messages for these modern times!

Acknowledgments

I wish to express, most of all, my love and appreciation to my wife, Marilyn, for the many days of patience, love, and kindness she extends to me, especially during those times when I attempt to work on the Kingdom's agenda.

I am grateful to my two sons: Larry Lawrence Jr., a young writer in his own right, and Minister Daniel Lawrence, my now thirteen-year-old preacher.

My thanks go also to the finest parents a preacher could be blessed with, parents who raised me in the tradition of the Christian faith. I can never repay my father, Louis Macon, and my mother, Delina Macon, for the kind of Christian atmosphere and love they provided as I grew up in the Cincinnati and Cleveland areas. I and all of my brothers and sisters were touched by God through these two angels sent from heaven.

I wish to thank all of the contributors, especially Dr. Henry J. Payden, Sr., my pastor; Dr. Otis Moss, Jr., Dr. Marvin A. McMickle, and Dr. William H. Myers, my mentors; and Rev. C. J. Matthews, Rev. Rodney Maiden, and Rev. Larry L. Harris, my peers.

My appreciation goes also to two friends I grew up with, Emery Ivery and Larry Griffin, who constantly challenged me to continue achieving and struggling in the works of the Lord.

As always, I wish to thank the members and friends of the Mt. Zion Baptist Church of Oakwood Village, Ohio, for their love, patience, prayers, and the many privileges they extend to me on a daily basis. Pastoring them is always a genuine thrill.

Finally, to the editorial staff of Kendall/Hunt Publishers, who have the highest of journalistic standards. For this I am grateful.

Contributors

Larry L. Macon, Sr. is pastor of Mt. Zion Baptist Church in Oakwood Village, a suburb of Cleveland, Ohio. He holds degrees from Cleveland State University (B.A.), and Ashland Theological Seminary (M.A. and D.Min.). He is the president of the United Pastors in Mission, an interdenominational pastoral group in Cleveland. Dr. Macon is the author of *Discipling the African American Male: How to Get Men into Church and Keep Them There* (Winston-Derek Publishers).

Otis Moss, Jr. is pastor of Olivet Institutional Baptist Church in Cleveland, Ohio. He obtained his B.A. degree from Morehouse College, his M.Div. degree from Morehouse School of Religion/Interdenominational Theological Center, and his D.Min. degree from United Theological Seminary in Dayton, Ohio. Dr. Moss has preached and lectured throughout the world. He serves as social justice executive officer of the United Pastors in Mission.

Marvin A. McMickle is pastor of the Antioch Baptist Church in Cleveland, Ohio. He is chairman of the United Pastors in Mission. He received a B.A. degree from Aurora College (Illinois), an M.Div. from Union Theological Seminary (New York), a D.Min. from Princeton Theological Seminary (New Jersey), and a Ph. D. from Case Western Reserve University in Cleveland. Dr. McMickle is the former president of several chapters of the NAACP.

Albert T. Rowan is pastor of the Bethany Baptist Church in Cleveland, Ohio. He holds a Th.B from Webster Baptist Bible College, an M.Div. from Ashland Theological Seminary, and a D.Min. from Trinity Theological Seminary. Dr. Rowan has held revivals across the United States, and is an esteemed pastor in America.

Sterling Glover has preached and taught across America for several decades. He earned his B.A. degree from Rutgers and his Th.M. degree from the American Divinity School in New York. He obtained a doctorate in Systematic Theology from Miller University. Rev. Glover is pastor of the historic Emmanuel Baptist Church in Cleveland, Ohio.

Rodney Maiden serves as pastor of the Providence Baptist Church in Cleveland, Ohio. He has a B.A. degree from Moody Bible Institute in Chicago. Rev. Maiden is a sought-after lecturer and speaker.

Richard E. Barnes is an ordained minister in the University Church of Christ, Cleveland, Ohio. He holds a B.A. degree in Religion and a Master's degree from the Cleveland State University. He has done work in the New Testament Studies of the historical Jesus and Pauline Epistles.

Timothy M. James is an ordained minister of the Disciples of Christ Church and serves as pastor of the Fifth Christian Church, Cleveland, Ohio. He received a B.A. degree from Culver-Stockton College, an M.Div. degree from Christian Theological Seminary, and a D.Min. degree from United Theological Seminary.

Larry Lawrence Harris is pastor of the Mt. Olive Baptist Church in Cleveland, Ohio. He obtained his B.A. degree from Duke University. Rev. Harris is well known for his illustrative sermons.

C. Jay Matthews serves as pastor of the distinguished Mt. Sinai Baptist Church in Cleveland, Ohio. He earned an M.A. degree from Ashland Theological Seminary and is a candidate for the D.Min. degree at Ashland Theological Seminary. He is the president of the SCLC, Cleveland Chapter.

Henry James Payden, Sr. is pastor of the Holy Trinity Baptist Church. He holds a B.A. degree from Capital University and an M.A. degree from Ashland Theological Seminary. He is certified in Clinical Psychology and Pastoral Counseling. He is nationally known for singing with the Wings Over Jordan. Rev. Payden is a preacher/teacher *par excellence.*

William H. Myers holds degrees from Cleveland State University (B.B.A.), Ashland Theological Seminary (M.A. and D.Min.), and University of Pittsburgh (Ph.D.). He has published essays and articles in a variety of journals and publications. His writings include *The Irresistible Urge to Preach: A Collection of African American*

"Call" Stories (Aaron Press), as well as *God's Yes Was Louder Than My No: Rethinking the African American Call to Ministry* (Eerdman's Publishing Company).

Andrew Edwards is pastor of Fellowship Missionary Baptist Church, Cleveland, Ohio. He obtained degrees from William Jewell College (B.A.), University of Kansas (M.S.W.), Ashland Theological Seminary (M.Div.), and Kansas State University (Ph.D.). Dr. Edwards is editor of *Human Services and Social Change: An African-American Church Perspective* (Orange Blossom Press), and is the author of several articles.

It Is Finished!

John 19:30

Larry L. Macon, Sr.

Let us take a journey back to Calvary, the hill called "Skull," the "place of Death." Jesus had been hanging on the cross for six hours. He was tired. His body was weak. The crowd ridiculed him. The people talked about him. He was somewhat delirious, for every bone had been shaken out of place. The blood dripping from the crown of thorns on his head and the stripes on his back had dried. He was tired! It became dark on Calvary, so dark that one could cut the darkness with a knife. With his body tired and weak, out of nowhere, yet from somewhere, he mounted enough energy to raise his body up on the nails, and cried in a trembling voice, **"It is finished!"**

A song writer looked at this Calvary event from the distance of time and asked, "Were you there when they crucified my Lord? Sometimes, it causes me to tremble, tremble, tremble." And Jesus cried with a loud voice, **"It is finished!"** These words of Jesus were familiar to those who stood around the cross. They had heard artists who had worked long and hard trying to perfect their paintings yell in exhilarated voices, "It's finished!" The farmer of their day, after working all year long planting seed and then during the time of harvest reaping what had been planted, would exclaim, "It's finished!" They had heard the priest, after examining the sacrifice or the sacrificial lamb and seeing it was without blot or blemish, affirm, "It is finished!"

So the people of Jesus' day heard this phrase, "It is finished," time and time again. Though it was a familiar phrase, it had different meaning to various people. To the soldiers who stood around the cross guarding the three malefactors, the shout of Jesus meant the end of a day's work. Their job was finished, and they could now forget this crucifixion as they had forgotten the hundreds of others. "It is finished!" To Mary, his mother, it meant her sorrow and grief were complete, for her son was dead. "It is finished!" To Pilate, the governor, it meant that even though his conscience would continue to accuse him, the threat to his authority by the Jews was now over! To Annas, Caiphas, and the other religious leaders, it meant that the threat to their establishment was now over, and the undermining influence of this "ghetto" preacher from Nazareth had now ended. These religious leaders could now return to their "status quo" and "business as usual" formats. To the crowd, it meant that the excitement of the day was over, and they could return home. To his disciples and friends, it meant the end of their hope! Yes, they were hoping that Jesus was the Promised Messiah, the Savior of Israel, and the Son of God. But they thought perhaps they were wrong. It is because of this sixth statement on the cross , "It is finished," that Peter and the other disciples may have decided they could now go back to fishing, for it was now over.

Well, the question that needs to be asked and explored is, what then is really finished? What did Jesus really mean when he cried, "It is finished." Is there not a theological emphasis behind these words?

The Completion of Types and Symbols

First of all, this cry of Jesus suggests the completion of the dispensation of types and symbols:

- ✝ Adam was a type of Christ because he came directly from God.

- ✝ Milchisedek was a type of Christ because he was without beginning or ending.

- ✝ Isaac was a type of Christ because he was offered on the altar of sacrifice.

- ✝ Joseph was a type of Christ because he was despised by his brothers.

- ✝ Solomon was a type of Christ because of his wisdom.

✝ Joshua was a type of Christ because of his tearing down the walls of Jericho.

✝ Sampson was a type of Christ because he carried off the gate of impossibilities.

✝ Jonah was a type of Christ because he was thrown into the midst of the sea to save others from destruction.

All of these were a type of Christ! Also, the high priest of the Jews, in the performance of every function pertaining to his priestly office, was a type of Christ. The priests' responsibilities included sprinkling of the sacrificial blood, offering the sacrifice on the altar, and entering into the Holy of Holies. Jesus became our High Priest. Therefore, when Jesus cried out, "It is finished," it was his way of saying all these types and symbols are now finished and completed in him.

Jesus took all of these rites and types of symbols with him to the cross. He, in essence, nailed them there. They died with him. They were buried with him. But when he rose from the grave, they didn't rise with him. That's why Matthew reported in his Gospel account, regarding the post-crucifixion event, that the veil of the temple was rent in two from the top to the bottom. Why? Because "It is finished!" Hence, these words are great words! They are the greatest words ever uttered, in the greatest moment of history, by the greatest person who ever lived on earth, announcing the greatest fact to the greatest number of people in time. These words bring the greatest blessing to the greatest multitude on earth and in heaven.

The Debt of Sin Is Paid

Secondly, not only are the types and symbols of Christ finished, but the debt of sin is now paid! Humankind was deep in debt through sin and its deadly power. Sinful man is in terrifying debt and man cannot pay out. But on the cross, bearing our sins in his own body, Jesus paid the debt! Elvina M. Hall in her hymn, "Jesus Paid It All," captures this thought poignantly:

> Jesus paid it all,
>
> All to Him I owe;
>
> Sin had left a crimson stain.
>
> He washed it white as snow.

This thought is further expressed in the story told whereby a little boy ran up to a preacher after Sunday service and pulled on the minister's coattail and asked, "Reverend, what can I do to be saved?" The preacher responded, "Nothing, because Jesus paid it all!"

"It is finished," said Christ. The great mission that Jesus came to do was now finished. Salvation was complete. He could now say, "It is finished!" When Jesus uttered these words, the earth's continents reeled. The earth's mountains bowed. Lebanon shook its frosty top and all its cedars groaned, the granite split, and the limestone oracles of Machpelah's cave split and shivered and threatened to crush the finer dust of the bones where they laid Abraham. In other words, when Jesus cried, "It is finished," God's Holy Ghost's spine was tickled, and the whole earth got happy and did a holy dance! Why? Because sin is finished!

His Work Is Complete

Thirdly, something had been accomplished! Jesus had dealt with the transgression of humankind and made reconciliation for iniquity and sin. He had purchased everlasting righteousness and sealed up the vision. When beginning his ministry, he said, "I must be about my Father's business" (Luke 2:49). Now he has finished the transaction, and soon he will proclaim triumph. His work is completed! Redemption is completed! The abolishment of death as penalty for every believer is accomplished. True, the Christian dies, but his and her death is no longer penal, but providential and provisional.

The great mission on which our Lord came to earth was finished. The hour for which he came into the world had run its course. And so he says: "I have placed the capping stone in Zion. I can rest my case now because the sin debt is paid in full." Envision and hear him as he cries with a loud voice, "IT IS FINISHED!" It was another way of saying to his Father: "Father, you can get my mansion ready. Father, get my crown ready. I've paid the debt in full and so it is finished! Father, get my chariot ready. Father, dust my throne off in glory because the final triumph has finally been made. The last nail has been driven and the case is now closed. The loose ends are now tied up and the rough places are chiseled out. Father, it's finished. Mission completed! I've fought a good fight and I've finished my course. I'm now ready to be offered up. **IT IS FIN-ISHED!**"

ather, Into Thy Hands I Commend My Spirit

Luke 23:46

Otis Moss, Jr.

It is an arresting thought to recognize how Jesus addressed God as "Father." "Father"—that's personal. "Father"—that's intimate. "Father"—that's family and foundational. "Father"—that brings to us more than social security, but soul security. "Father"—that eliminates the ultimate sense of homelessness. "Father"—in the true sense of the expression, indicates that I have a home. "Father"— that's beyond Armageddon. "Father, into Thy hands I commend my spirit," according to Luke. And Jesus addressed God in terms of a parent, in terms of a personal image, and in terms of an intimate and personal relationship whereby Jesus opens a door for each of us in the familyhood of God. You and I can now go to our parent who is God!

With an intimate and personal relationship with a parent, we can overcome the world. You can call on your parent. Do you remember, growing up, when something went wrong? When an older child or another child in the neighborhood threatened you? Your ultimate appeal was to go home and tell your parent, and the ultimate authority was to tell your father. Edwina and I have been blessed in our home with children. In our parental memory system we computerized our children's calls. So when one calls and says, "Dad" or "Mom," we know who it is. And based upon the rhythm, the melody, or the pathos in their voice, we can almost tell what the trouble is. So there are times when we respond to the request with a "yes" and other times when we say "no." Sometimes, we ask,

7

"What's wrong?" "What is it?" Everybody needs to be able to address and attach themselves to an intimate and personal God to whom you can go in confidence and know that your confidence will not be violated!

"Father"—that's a powerful expression of God! "Father, the hour has come," says Jesus. Matthew, in the model prayer, writes, "Lord, teach us to pray." "And when you pray say, 'Our Father.'" On another occasion Jesus said, "Father, if it be possible let this cup pass." You are my parent and I am your son, and whatever the father wills, the son will do. "Into thy hands I commend my spirit."

In my college days, one of the most profound personalities I had the benefit of meeting was a rather quiet hero. Not much is known or said about him these days. He was in one sense a country farmer. He went to the University of Georgia and graduated with a degree in agriculture. He continued his graduate work at the Southern Baptist Theological Seminary where he majored in New Testament Studies, specializing in Greek. But this Georgia country farmer, with a degree in agriculture and an advanced degree in New Testament Studies and Greek, also had a background in the southern soil of segregation and racism. In Georgia, he organized what was known as the "Koinonia Farm," and decided to organize a lifestyle for all people on that farm of some eleven hundred acres to model that of the church in the Acts of the Apostles.

This farmer and New Testament scholar made sure that the doors to this farm were open to everyone, regardless of race or color. This was a long time before the 1954 Supreme Court decision on desegregation or the sit-ins or the civil rights movement. This was before the leadership in Montgomery Bus Boycott and Rosa Parks. It was before Martin Luther King's leadership and his Birmingham jail cell, or Dr. T. J. Jemerson's boycott in Baton Rouge. It was before Thurgood Marshall had opened the door to the Supreme Court. The Ku Klux Klan often visited the farm. They tried to run Clarence Jordan and all of his associates out of the county, near Americus, Georgia. Clarence Jordan tells the story of how one night, about 1:30 a.m., the telephone rang. He picked up the phone and someone on the other end of the line asked, "Is this Clarence Jordan?" Clarence Jordan responded, "Yes." The voice then said, "Well, I want you to know that in a few minutes, a green pickup truck will come over from the bridge and turn on the car lights in the driveway; you have about seventeen minutes to get all of the people out of your house. It will be at that time that dynamite will begin to explode." Clarence Jordan said, "Well, who are you?" The strange caller responded, "That's not important. I just wanted you to know." Dr. Jordan then said, "With this kind of information, won't you at least let me know who you are so that I can express my gratitude?" The voice on the other end of the line said, "I told you, that's not important. Now you've got sixteen minutes."

Clarence Jordan hung up the phone. His son had awakened, and he asked his daddy what that was all about. Clarence Jordan said, "Oh, someone says they're going to blow up the place in sixteen minutes." His son said, "Oh," and turned over and went back to sleep. Clarence Jordan went back to the bedroom and his wife asked, "What were you talking about?" He said, "Well, honey, someone said they're going to blow up this place in about fifteen minutes." She said, "Really?" and turned over and went to sleep. The Jordan family had been threatened so often and so long over the years that they had become immune to the threats. They had learned to fear no evil. But Clarence Jordan says he couldn't go back to sleep. Sure enough, as the clock kept ticking away, he heard a truck pull up to the house in the darkness. Finally, the lights came on and he wondered in fear what to do. Then, he decided to go back to bed. He said to himself, "If God wants to use us tonight as a living sacrifice and as a sin bearer, then I'm going back to bed and leave it in the hands of God. If this is not to be, it's in God's hands. But if it is to be, I'm not going to be caught in the night running up and down the yard in my pajamas. I'm going back to bed and go to sleep!"

The next morning, Clarence Jordon and his family awoke, still in the land of the living. His tongue was not cleaved to the roof of his mouth. He had the activity of his limbs. When he said, "Good morning," the whole household responded, "Good morning!" What did Clarence Jordan do? He simply went to bed that night and said, "Father, into Thy hands I commend my spirit."

When the world is threatening you and incurable diseases have invaded your body, when you have to stand alone on some Isle of Patmos, when you have to bear your cross and even your intimate family does not seem to quite understand the power of the threat that has come your way—then my advice is for you to go to sleep in God's name and rest your case! We must learn to say, "Father, into Thy hands I commend my spirit."

Finally, we must ask the question, "Why are you going to commend your spirit in God's hands, Jesus?" His response would be, "Well, It's the best thing I can do. I can't leave my spirit in the hands of Simon Peter because when the going gets rough he will forget who I am. He will forget that I fed the five thousand. He will deny me. I can't leave my spirit in the hands of John the Baptist, though he was a good friend and family member, because on the right day he will ask the wrong question. I can't leave my spirit in the hands of David. Although his sword is sharp and his slingshot is accurate, and he is a king after God's own heart, there are too many contradictions in his life. I can't leave my spirit in the hands of Solomon. He has too many primary wives and far too many secondary wives to take charge of my spirit. I can't leave my spirit in the hands of home folk for they are still wondering, 'Can any good thing come out of Nazareth?'" I can't leave my spirit even in the hands of my mother, Mary, because she'll want me to go home with her, when I must be about my Father's business. I can't leave my spirit in the hands of Adam and Eve, Cain or Abel; or Abraham and Sarah, Isaac and Jacob. I cannot leave my spirit in the hands of the right wing or the left wing, Democrats or Republicans! But, Father, into Thy hands I commend my spirit. The reason I'm going to leave my spirit in God's hands is because I can call God up when I need Him! I'm going to leave my spirit with my Father. Then on Pentecost Day, my spirit will come back in a double measure. I'm leaving my spirit in my Father's hands. Then on the Isle of Patmos, my disciple, John, can be caught up in the spirit on the Lord's Day. My spirit is in the Father's hands. Therefore, the best that you and I can do is to leave everything in the hands of God, our Father. *Father, into Thy hands I commend my Spirit!*"

Testimony of the Tortured

Acts 16:35

Marvin A. McMickle

Here is a story and an example of faith under pressure. Though the message may seem subtle to the ear of the listener, its message speaks loudly to the faith of any believer. The story deals with the behavior of Paul and Silas while confined in a maximum-security prison in the city of Philippi. So often we hear about these verses without fully understanding everything that was involved in this scene. However, when the text is analyzed more deeply, one can then understand the extraordinary series of events which occurred that night.

Allow me to point out several things in this text and then focus on each of them at some length. I want us to first notice who is in the text and the unusual hour during which the story occurs. Secondly, we will look into what they were doing at that time and in that place. Thirdly, we will deal with their act of faithfulness which resulted in three distinct things, none of which would have happened had Paul and Silas not remained faithful to God.

The two lead characters in the text are Paul and Silas. We know a great deal about Paul. He was the Evangelist of the Christian faith. After his conversion on the road between Jerusalem and Damascus, Paul engaged in a series of three missionary journeys. During this time he spread the message of Jesus Christ throughout Palestine, Asia Minor, and southern Europe. This text finds the Apostle Paul traveling from Jerusalem through parts of Asia on his second missionary journey. Traveling with him was Silas. We do not know as much about Silas as we do about Paul. Most scholars agree that

Silas was the Hebrew name of a man who is also known as Silavanus in II Corinthians 1:19. He was a leader of the Christian church in Jerusalem, selected by Paul to travel along with him after Paul and Barnabas had a feud over the role that John Mark should play as an Evangelist. From that point on Barnabas traveled with Mark while Paul traveled with Silas. It was during their travels together that Paul and Silas found themselves imprisoned at Philippi. Not only were both of these men Jews who converted to Christianity, but it seems as though they were also Roman citizens. Please keep this in mind as the story unfolds.

Paul has had a vision during the night in which he apparently heard the voice of a man saying, "Come over to Macedonia and help us." Paul perceives this as a call to spread the gospel in that part of the world. Therefore, he and Silas travel to that region. Soon after their arrival they meet a woman possessed by some evil spirit. This spirit has given her the ability to tell the future and to reveal mysteries. She is the slave of a group of men in Philippi who have become rich by charging people to have their futures told. Paul and Silas cast out the spirit in her and, in so doing, take away the source of profit for those men. In anger, they falsely accuse Paul and Silas of spreading religious teachings that had been outlawed in Roman colonies like Philippi. Based upon this false accusation, Paul and Silas are subjected to almost unimaginable brutality. They are stripped naked, publicly whipped, beaten, and then cast into the most secure part of the prison. Then they are chained to the wall by their neck, hands, and feet. The effect of this is not simply that Paul and Silas are punished for robbing those men of their source of income; of far more importance is the fact that their missionary journey seems to have been halted. The power of a Roman judge appears to have frustrated the will of God and hindered the gospel message.

Praying and Singing

It is uncertain how much time passes, but this much is known: Paul and Silas have been falsely accused and brutally beaten. In the sixteenth chapter of the book of Acts, the writer says they were beaten with many stripes. They were then locked into a bleak and unlit dungeon. This we know because at the hour of midnight, they turned that dark dungeon into a sanctuary. The dungeon echoed with the sound of their prayers and songs of praise. They have been beaten, battered, and left bleeding. They were chained to a wall in this Roman prison. They could have been downhearted and dejected. Their missionary journey, which began with such hope and promise, now seemed so hopeless. Who knew if they would ever come out of that prison alive! Who could have blamed them if they complained about their condition? That is what most people do when they suffer, whether that suffering is undeserved or not. They would at the very least complain about their condition. "Why me, Lord?" "This is not fair, Lord!" "I don't deserve this, Lord!" When most people would be fussing, complaining, and feeling sorry for themselves, Paul and Silas were awake at midnight, praying and singing in their prison cell. These two men who had just been tortured still had a testimony of praise to God!

Notice also, that so far as Paul and Silas were concerned, there was no special time and place for prayer and singing. For them it made more sense to do their singing and praying when they were in the midst of troubles than to reserve it just for the formal times of worship. They were as ready to worship God in prison, at midnight, as they were in any church on a Sunday morning. These men did not let their tortures erase their testimony. Even though they were in prison, both of them were still able to focus on their faith and keep their eyes on Jesus!

I wonder how most of us would measure up against such a standard? I will acknowledge that most of us are willing and able to testify to our faith in church. Most of us are willing to sing and pray when we are in the sanctuary. Most of us are willing to sing and pray when we are in the company of the congregation. However, the real test of our faith is whether or not we are as likely to be heard singing and praying when we are away from the church—especially when we are in trouble. I believe that the best time for the songs of faith is not when we are seated in church, dressed up and smelling good. If we are the children of God, then somebody ought to hear us humming on our job. It is there that somebody ought to hear us humming, "The Lord will make a way somehow." If we are really children of God, somebody ought to hear us singing in our hospital room that "through it all, I've learned to trust in Jesus and I've learned to trust in God." If we are children of the most High God, somebody ought to hear us singing when our children are in the police station. We ought to sing when our spouse is being lowered into a grave. Our song might be:

Precious Lord, take my hand, lead me on and let me
stand.

I am tired, I am weak, I am worn!

Through the storm, through the night, lead me on to
the light.

Take my hand, Precious Lord, and lead me on!

Paul and Silas in the Philippian jail, and John on the Island of
Patmos, had it right! The best time to sing is when you are in trouble!

Authentic Prayer

Not only is singing more encouraging when it is done while one is
in trouble, but prayer becomes more authentic. I do not believe that
people can learn how to pray until they have come up against a
problem which they cannot solve. Authentic prayer occurs when we
are up against burdens we cannot handle, or a need we cannot meet
on our own. You can hear people pray and just about tell whether
they have been through some time of torture, whether physical or
spiritual. Some people's prayers are so proper, it's as if they are
more interested in how they sound than in being heard by God. But
when one is in trouble or in the lion's den of life, and prays with an
urgency, then authentic prayer occurs. Here in the text, Paul and
Silas had been beaten and chained to a wall, and the only thing they
were concerned about was being heard by God.

The Audience

Notice, however, that Paul and Silas had an audience beyond God
as they sang and prayed in jail. Acts 16:25 gives this additional fact,
"... and the prisoners heard them." Theirs becomes a powerful testimony when we realize that there is always somebody else nearby
who hears and sees us. The best time for us to sing and pray is not
only when we are in trouble, but also when the world is watching.
We need to let our light so shine before the world that they may see
our good works and glorify our Father in heaven.

I have often wondered what happened to those other prisoners who heard Paul and Silas. I wonder if any of them were converted that night? The text does not say. It says only what you and I need to know, and that is that the prisoners heard them. You or I may never know if anybody will ever come to know Christ because of anything we have said, but we do know that if they never hear us say anything, the chances of their being saved are reduced. Let the world hear us! What this text is setting before us today is that our best work as witnesses occurs when people overhear us when we pray and sing. Our best prayers are not at home or in church, but in restaurants, when other diners see us bow our head and give thanks for our meal. Paul and Silas prayed and sang in that Philippian prison. The other prisoners heard them, and that is our challenge as well.

The next thing I want you to notice in this text is that when we are not sure whether anybody else hears our prayer, God certainly does. I really want to say this to those of you who are going through some difficulty while wondering if God hears, or worse, if God even cares. The testimony of this text is that God hears and answers prayer. Most biblical scholars agree that in this text the earthquake is not just a sudden event of nature. Instead, it is the way that God chose to respond to the prayers of Paul and Silas. There are no voices that speak or visions that come to them in the night. Consequently, God sets His servants free from their shackles and knocks open their prison doors.

Just when it looked as if their missionary work had come to an end, God answered their prayers. Paul and Silas were set free. And what a controlled earthquake it was: just enough to knock open the doors and break the shackles. Not even the ceiling or walls collapsed. God was not out to destroy the prison; He just wanted to set his servants free.

This is not the first time that God used power from the natural order to accomplish His purpose. When the people of Israel found themselves trapped at the Red Sea, with the army of Pharaoh racing in behind them and the rushing waves of the sea before them, God used the wind. The wind blew a path for his people in the midst of the waters so that Israel could pass through on dry ground. When the prophet Elijah ran away to avoid the wrath of Ahab and Jezebel, he found himself by a dry brook. God then sent a raven that brought Elijah food every day. God made the sun stand still for Joshua when he had a battle to fight. And as we have discovered in our study of Revelation, when God comes to judge the world at the end of time, He will work primarily through the elements of the natural order.

Over and over, Jesus demonstrated that he had power over the natural order. He could speak to a violent storm on the Sea of Galilee and cause the winds and waves to cease from their boisterous roaring and terrible raging. He could multiply fish and loaves, turn water into wine, heal the sick, and raise the dead. So when God used an earthquake to release Paul and Silas from their prison cell, it was simply another sign of the tremendous power that God used throughout biblical history. We need to know that when we are in trouble and face our trials, we are not left alone to rely on our own resources. We do not serve a God who is unable to come to our aid. Our God has power.

Are you facing a delicate and dangerous medical procedure? God has enough power to meet your need! Turn to God in faith and trust, even when you are going through a torturous situation like that of Paul and Silas. God is able to shake the earth around you and bring you out! That is what we learn from this text.   There is no place the world can send us where God cannot find us. There is no pain the world inflicts upon us that God cannot heal. There is no burden the world places upon us that God cannot help us bear. There is no sorrow of the world that God cannot soothe. God can wipe away our tears. There is no chain of addiction that God cannot shatter and set us free. It is good to know our God has power available to us, some of which he used that midnight when he broke the bonds of Paul and Silas.

Finally, notice that the missionary journey of Paul and Silas was to continue right in that prison. When the earthquake shook, it opened all the cells and set all the prisoners free. The jailer was about to kill himself. The Roman law operated on the principle that if anyone escaped from one of their prisons, the jailer in charge would pay either by being killed or by killing himself. He thought that all the prisoners had escaped during the commotion. Suddenly, Paul cried out to the jailer that he should not hurt himself. Paul informed the jailer that none of the prisoners had escaped. Realizing that the power of God had just been manifested, the Jailer cried out one of the most memorable lines in all the Bible, "What must I do to be saved?" That question is then answered by both Paul and Silas, who say to him, "Believe on the Lord Jesus Christ and you shall be saved, and all your household." That very same hour the jailer confessed his faith in Christ. Then, something almost unimaginable occurred. First the jailer took Paul and Silas into his house and got water to cleanse their wounds. He may have helped to apply the stripes to their back but he was now washing them in his own home. Then the text records that he was baptized. I wonder with what he was baptized? I wonder if that same blood-stained water used to wipe their wounds was then water used to wipe away his sins? It brings to mind one of the strange and compelling images of Christian theology, namely, that sins can be washed clean through the use of blood. Robert Lowery, a songwriter, one day asked the question:

What can wash away my sins?

Nothing but the blood of Jesus;

What can make me whole again?

Nothing but the blood of Jesus.

Oh! precious is the flow That makes me white as snow;

No other fount I know, Nothing but the blood of Jesus.

The Bible says that the jailer was saved and baptized. The work of spreading the gospel and bringing Gentiles into a knowledge of Christ was completed. Imprisonment could not stop it. The same message that Paul and Silas preached in that midnight prayer meeting in Philippi is available to us. We now have the privilege to declare it to the world today. This is the message of the church: "Believe on the Lord Jesus Christ and thou shalt be saved." This is what the Church must preach until Christ comes again. Let this be our testimony and we too will be blessed. Let us declare with unfailing faithfulness the Lordship of Christ and His power to save from sin. For "We have heard a joyful sound, Jesus saves, Jesus saves!"

It's Time to Talk

Acts 4:20

Albert T. Rowan

Much of what we hear in reference to talking has been negative, and so many have said, "Action speaks louder than words." Others have said, "If you want to discover a man's weak points, let him do all the talking while you do all the listening." Robert Benchley, the great American humorist, said, "And then, drawing upon my fine command of the English language, I said nothing." However, in spite of all the negative aspects of speaking, the Bible has something positive to say:

PSALM 17:1	"Let the words of my mouth, and the meditation of my heart be acceptable in thy sight, O Lord, my strength and my Redeemer."
PSALM 17:2	"Let the Redeemed of the Lord, say so."
PROVERBS 15:23	"A word spoken in due season, how good it is."
MATTHEW 12:36	"But I say unto you that every idle word that men shall speak, they shall give account thereof in the day of Judgment."

These and many other references in Scripture give us the importance of the spoken word as a powerful agent for the human tongue. The power of speech is a gift that stands eminent among the good gifts of God to His creatures. Speaking is man's most potent instrument for good over evil. The tongue of the statesman can bring blessings upon millions of people, but when it is made the tool of personal ambition, it may bring misery upon the generations to come.

We live in a fast world!—a world of TV sets, computers, microwave ovens, radios, and many other modern means of communication. The pace of our world is rapid! As we enter into night's rest, we are suddenly awakened to the sound of an alarm clock by way of a booming radio that gives to us the night's happenings while we were asleep. We can know what is happening "live" half way across the world through TV. We can leave Los Angeles today by jet plane, cross the international dateline, and arrive in Asia yesterday.

However, with all these modern means, we still suffer from a lack of real communication among the people of the world. With our modern means of travel, the world becomes a neighborhood. It has yet to become a brotherhood. And so it's important that we realize that IT'S TIME TO TALK!

In the early church, the disciples of our Lord Jesus Christ did not suffer from a lack of communication. They were able to move the world with the right talk. In the midst of their world filled with tyranny, oppression, and fears, they "turned the world right side up." How did they do this without modern means of communication? They simply told their story, which was exciting and full of wonder. Their story spread like wildfire from village to village and from town to town. Their words were so powerful that even the harsh commands of the organized religious leaders were disobeyed. Though it meant persecution, imprisonment, and in some cases death, the story continued being told, and those who heard it were so amazed in wonderment that they began to tell it also! They called it "good news," and indeed it was good news for a troubled and confused world. It is still good news today. This good news of the Gospel story needs to be rediscovered in our world today. The story is told of Peter and John, two of Jesus' closest disciples, who were insistent upon telling others about their new way of life in Christ. They could not help but tell what had happened to them, for they had not taken up their calling as a matter of choice, but in obedience to the impulse of their conscience. They had to speak regardless of the persecution and in spite of imprisonment. They had to speak because of their irresistible sense of duty to their new master who guided their hearts. They had seen and heard the Master, Himself, after His resurrection. He had commanded them like the many others who had embraced the new life in Christ to "Go and teach all nations, baptizing them in the name of the Father, the Son, and the Holy Ghost." They then realized that it was TIME TO TALK!

The Christian Church today has been called upon to speak words of hope and peace to humankind. Today's church must become a voice to reach the ears of this troubled generation. The great tragedy is that while the proponents of violence, oppression, and fear are having their say, the church of Jesus Christ is silent. Others are speaking out on the subject of what's politically correct, what's economically profitable, what's good for our nation and world, while the subject of the goodness of God remains a silent issue. The church has become so complacent. It's time to talk about our God and Lord Jesus Christ! He is the world's only hope!

It's time to talk to and about our young people. The youth of today will be our leaders of tomorrow and we must begin to help them acquire habits of devotion to God that will fit them for many of the great tasks that lie ahead. It is also time for Christian youth to talk and impact their peers for Jesus. Many are predicting that today's youth will fill tomorrow's jails, that they are a wild and unruly group. Yet, many fail to see that there are Christian youth who are preparing today to lead in a better tomorrow. Many are also giving their hearts to Christ and accepting the challenge to minister to a lost and dying world. Others are trying to be soldiers in the army of the Lord. And they are letting the world know that they have something to say and refuse to allow others to be the only ones talking.

Also, IT'S TIME TO TALK about the goodness in this world. All is not lost and we do have hope. The thing that impresses me more and more as I go through this life and meet people is not so much that there is trouble in the world, but how much goodness exists. We know that Satan is busy, but he is losing the war. What about the goodness in the world? There are so many dedicated Christians in the world. In the Bible the story is told of a Good Samaritan. It does not surprise me that two men passed by on the other side of the road while their neighbor suffered, but let's not forget that there is the Good Samaritan who took time out to help the stranger on the roadside who had been beaten. Good things are happening every day, things that we will never read about in the newspapers or hear on the radio. Well, it's time we said something about the goodness of our world. IT'S TIME TO TALK!

It's time for us to talk about our Christian witness. We have some good news about the Christ who lived and died and rose again! It's good news that is too good to keep. Have you realized that as followers of the Lord, we have the panacea for the ills of the world? Have you realized that Christ is too glorious to hide? The Christian of today is called upon to hold the line or keep the territory we have gained. We are called upon to break into new soil and dare the hazards of the untrodden road! We need to blaze a trail for the future. IT'S TIME TO TALK!

But some will say, "Well, I don't count for anything. I'm only one voice. How can I contribute anything when there is so much to say?" Be certain that ONE MAKES A DIFFERENCE!

One additional electoral vote would have made Aaron Burr the president of the United States in America.

One vote permitted Texas to be brought into the United States.

One vote saved President Andrew Jackson from being impeached.

One person, Joan of Arc, saved France from defeat and domination.

One preacher, Savanorola, changed Florence, Italy.

One leader, Martin Luther, altered the course of western history by tacking the 95 theses for debate on the door of Wittenburg's All Saints Church that started the Protestant Reformation period.

One shoemaker, William Carey, persisted in going with the gospel to India and launched the modern missionary movement.

One black Baptist preacher, Martin Luther King, Jr., changed the social atmosphere of the United States of America.

One black woman, Rosa Parks, refused to give up her seat on a bus in Montgomery, Alabama, and started the Civil Rights Movement.

One is IMPORTANT! Listen:

One mischievous child can break up a school.

One false alarm can cause a panic.

One match can start a huge forest fire.

One false step can cost a life or ruin a character.

One broken wheel can ditch a train.

One quarrelsome worker can create a strike by thousands.

One undiplomatic word can provoke a war involving thousands of lives and the destruction of millions of dollars in property.

One wayward son can break a mother's heart.

One lie can destroy a person's character.

One false witness can send an innocent man to jail.

One drink can start a person on the road to alcoholism.

One large leak can sink the Titanic.

One broken link can make a chain useless.

But, one kind word at the right time can save a person from suicide. One sermon may fire many a person's soul and set the course of his or her future life! One plus one is the story of the Bible. God plus Abraham and God plus Moses. God plus one committed person have kept the torch of faith burning. You may be only one, and you may seem insignificant. You may even be inclined to dismiss yourself as worthless. But with God you are important! IT'S TIME TO TALK!

You have a story to tell, and only you can tell it! If you've been blessed, you must no longer hide the splendid facts. You must recite them, publish them, and as far as possible, let all the world know. And so, if you have the love of God in your heart, if you are trusting Christ for salvation, if you believe in His word, if you are trying to do His will and know that you have a mansion waiting in Heaven, then you ought to tell somebody. IT'S TIME TO TALK!

You would tell somebody if you bought a beautiful new home or automobile. You would tell someone if you received a great hon-

or. If you lay claim to salvation according to the Scripture. If you know Christ as a personal savior, then IT'S TIME TO TALK!

May God give you the courage to tell your story. When you begin to tell it, you will embark upon an adventure that is too thrilling to miss!

> If you cannot sing like angels
>
> If you cannot preach like Paul,
>
> You can tell of the love of Jesus,
>
> You can say He died for all.

"For we cannot but speak of the things we have seen and heard." TELL SOMEBODY!

iberation Thru the Cross

Luke 4:18-19; I Cor. 1:18

Sterling E. Glover

How great and how noble is man since he has come of age. Our world shows evidence of his brilliance. His technology has reduced his travel time between continents. His slide rule and computers have built him large industrial camps and beautiful sprawling cities and suburbs. Someone went so far as to suggest that "if we will only use our heads and play it right, we'll soon have a way of life that will make religion and the church no longer necessary."

I think this last statement gives to us the key to our modern human predicament. Our civilization was forged into such an existence through similar ideas by those who were pioneers for what is now called this modern age. They too had their denials of nature's God, a kind of moving away from the fact that the Eternal has a personal investment in this house of clay. Such movement only leads to servitude to our base nature. As of late, the great eternities of heaven and hell have been denied by many and the God of the universe overlooked!

Now, our theme of liberation suggests that while on planet earth man is chained to materialistic concepts, bogged down within himself and a prisoner of his own self-centeredness of worshiping the idol of secularism. However, fear and self-annihilation stalk humanity's footsteps. Man is said to have no other existence than biological on this horizontal plane in this context called earth. He thinks total happiness is gained through pleasure and the making of money. Yet, he soon discovers that pleasure with money does not automatically guarantee happiness. Therefore, mankind has turned to other saviors for salvation, only to find that they are weak and bring temporary satisfaction.

Man has turned to PSYCHOLOGY! However, even in the field of psychology there are flaws. Arthur Koestler suggested: "During the last explosive stages of the evolution of *homo sapiens*, something has gone wrong. There is a flaw, some subtle engineering mistake built into our native equipment which accounts for the paranoid streak running through our history." B. F. Skinner, author of the book entitled *Beyond Freedom and Dignity*, points out that the entire problem of man's behavior lies in the external influences that affect him daily. Skinner is of the opinion that if you change the environment by creating better social systems, man's psychological problems would be eliminated. He suggested that the environment needs to be changed by creating better schools and removing economic chains of oppression. Then, man's psychological pains could be removed, and there would be no sense of selfishness, greediness, unloving, or arrogance.

However, I believe that this utopian philosophy is self-destructive and dangerous because it allows man to rebuke himself with the tools of egoism and an arrogance that our 20th century alone has proven to be unworkable. Man is already like a top, spinning unto himself, ready to topple. He needs a real sense of balance.

Moreso, mankind has turned to TECHNOLOGY for the answer. Yet, technology's fingers have become tainted with the odor of perversion, gadgets, and instruments which have a way of leading us into death and destruction—so much so that their creators and inventors cringe with mortal fear before these very same gadgets. Scientists are screaming, "It's minutes into midnight!" We are about to be destroyed through biological warfare. After surveying our technological stockpiles, an American scientist said, "Now it is possible to destroy the human race in a single day." A Canadian scientist added, "No, all of humankind in a single minute!"

Seemingly, all of our advancements have only produced a numbed and wearied age with its madness to rush into nowhere. Magazine advertisements cry, "Are you tired?" and then offer to this weary, harassed generation a great galaxy of cures that are no real cures! Isn't it strange how we who possess more labor- saving devices than ever before are really the ones dragging our feet in weariness! Really, it's not our feet that are merely tired, and it is not our tired blood, but our spirits that are bound and our hearts that are failing in fear.

There is something morally dead about our society. Our moral and mental skies are so overcast, we can't see for looking. As Norman Pittenger affirms: "We are children lost in a haunted forest! We are afraid of our own world while most of us are frustrated and fearful. Most of us have only slim hopes of a better tomorrow. We are impotent, while lack of meaning has become a constant companion." Modern man is imprisoned in the mind without doors of access and windows of release. I'm convinced that all the enjoyment he gets out of this life is a defeating attempt at psychoanalyzing the worries that go on within his strange personality. He is like an egg that can be broken in two ways, either from the outside or from the inside. Yet, he is constantly broken.

But as a preacher of God and a "voice in the wilderness," I suggest that he allow himself to be broken, from within or without, and allow the chick on the inside to emerge. There is something on the inside that wants to come forth! And just like the chicken, he must slowly allow it to pick away so as to come forth and discover a new world. Once this chick emerges and picks his way through the shell of a difficult world, if he uses his instinct right, he can discover a bigger and broader world than the mere confines of the shell. Given the greater environment, the chicken can begin the laborious task of hooking up to that which is beyond itself! Thus, true liberation will occur.

Let me then suggest what true liberation is not! It is not getting to Mars first and establishing a real estate sales office or the largest armed force service in the universe on that planet. It is not establishing a civil religion called Americanism. No, liberation goes deeper than the confines of consciousness and unconsciousness. Out of the subconsciousness flow the heart's thought patterns of life. But way down deep in the soul, we are either on our way to heaven or hell, saved or lost. As Nicodemus asked our Lord, "How can these things be?" Evolution answers this perplexing question of Nicodemus by concluding that Genesis gives an account of four levels of existence: chemical, plant, animal, and mankind, and the movement is upward. If anything lower is ever to mount to a higher plane, two conditions are required: First of all, the higher must come down to the lower in order for there to be a descent from that which is above. Secondly, that which is lower must surrender its lower existence to that which is higher. For example, it is possible for the rain and the phosphates and the carbon to enter the higher life of the plant. But to do so, the plant must go down into the earth in search of these life giving nourishments. The plant says to these elements, "Unless you die to your lower existence, you cannot live in my kingdom of the plant life." Yet, if the plants are to live in the animal kingdom, then the animal life must come down to the plant life and snatch the plants through the grinding jaws of death. Hence, we must say to the plant: "Do you want to live up here in this animal life existence? If so, then you must die to your lower existence and become flesh of my flesh and bones of my bones." The plant then becomes a part of a living thing endowed with five senses.

Now when mankind, in his turn, takes chemicals, plants, and animals into his nature, he too must say, "Unless you die you cannot live up here in my human kingdom. You cannot be a part of my thinking, willing, and loving abilities unless you die to yourself. You cannot become a part of the world of poetry, philosophy, theology, culture, or Christianity."

But man was made for an existence beyond himself which leads to real liberation! He is to be a child of the highest! And to make this leap from time to eternity, God the creator has to come down in the form of mankind. I've got some real good news of liberation! He's come down in human flesh, for flesh. The higher has descended to the lower, so that the lower may ascend unto the higher. He came by way of Jesus Christ, who still stands in 20th-century time declaring, "You must be born again in order to move up into my Kingdom which is not of this world." He still says, "You must give up your earthly existence and sense of what's civilized and cultured." But too many of us don't want to die to our lower selves because it costs too much. Yet, liberation is expensive, and Jesus Christ still cries: "But as many as received Him to them gave he power to become the sons of God." Liberation becomes a process and new creation begins! Jesus Christ still shouts through the channels of time declaring power!

> "For the Spirit of the Lord is upon me. He has anointed me to preach the gospel to the poor, to liberate those who are in chains. He has sent me to heal the brokenhearted, to preach deliverance to the captives and recovering of sight to the blind, to set a liberty to them that are bruised, to preach the acceptable year of the Lord." (Luke 4:18-19)

But this same Jesus declares: "It's got to be done my way!" Therefore, His paradoxical cross becomes the instrument of liberation. For all who believe on the death, burial, and resurrection shall be saved or liberated! Because Jesus and the cross are synonymous with Good News! For the cross is the heartbeat of the gospel.

OUT YONDER: Something dramatic and far reaching was going on!

OUT YONDER: Behind the drop of nature, the Son of God was negotiating the contract of liberation!

OUT YONDER: Jesus gathered all of Adam's sins and bore them in His body upon the cross and "HE WHO KNEW NO SIN BECAME SIN FOR US!"

OUT YONDER: The seed of the woman was bruised!

OUT YONDER: He was wounded for our transgressions and bruised for our iniquities!

OUT YONDER: Mercy and Peace kissed each other!

OUT YONDER: The gate of the hog's pen was thrown open so prodigals everywhere could throw away their husk and partake of the Bread of Life and shout, I'm a Child of the King!"

And the songwriter declared:

> On a hill far away stood an old rugged cross,
> The emblem of suffering and shame;
> And I love that old cross where the dearest and best
> For a world of lost sinners was slain.
>
> So I'll cherish the old rugged cross,
> Till my trophies at last I lay down;
> I will cling to the old rugged cross,
> And exchange it some day for a crown.

Charge to Keep

Matthew 20:18-20

Rodney Maiden

The Great Commission is the magnificent obsession of the Church. It is the heartbeat of the church and the very life blood of Christendom itself. When we cease to dream, we cease to live. The steps from "risk takers" to "care takers" is but a short step to "undertaker." We need the Great Commission!

In a day in which millions are plunging into eternity without Christ, there is the danger of standing still and backing up. An automobile company has as its slogan, "We are driven!" As believers we too are driven. We are driven by our great commander-in-chief, Jesus Christ, to declare the Great Commission to the ends of the earth!

So profound were the experiences in the life of our Lord Jesus that it was impossible for one man to record and comprehend the full magnitude of His ministry. Therefore, the Holy Spirit assigned not one but four reporters to follow Him in the Gospel accounts. In examining the unique contribution of each reporter, we can gain insight into the fullness of our Lord's earthly ministry. Nowhere is this more true than in the various accounts of the Great Commission. Luke records two in his Gospel, the other in Acts. Though John recorded none, it is still true that there are four accounts of the Great Commission in the Gospels when you include Matthew's and Mark's accounts. Each account gives a different perspective, but when taken together, they comprise the whole. There is the account in Matthew 20:18-20 whereby the emphasis is placed on the words "in earth" (v. 18), "all nations" (v. 19), and the "end of the world" (v. 20). It is quite clear from Matthew's perspective that Jesus was emphasizing world penetration of the gospel. This is an inclusive clause whereby all nations, all cultures, all ethnic groups are to receive the message of the Great Commission. Matthew was a tax collector, a scribe, a bookkeeper, a statistician, an accountant, and a chronicler of events. Matthew shares with us his view that Jesus absolutely insisted on a "line upon line, precept upon precept" evangelism process. No stratum of society is to be excluded, no fortress of hell unpenetrated, no bastion of darkness is impregnable with the light of the gospel. Every religion must be confronted, every tribe invaded, every error exposed, every language translated, every city and hamlet, country and continent must be invaded until the foundations of hell tremble and Satan's walls crumble to the ground.

> For the darkness shall turn to dawning
>
> And the dawning to noonday bright!
>
> And Christ's great kingdom shall come on earth,
>
> The kingdom of love and light!

Mark's perspective of evangelizing everywhere and into all the world is a frightening thought. He, himself, is frightened during his early stage of evangelizing. He is different from the other reporters. Far from the status of a Roman official like Matthew, Mark was a nobody. Some have suggested him to be an older teenager or, at best, a young man in his early twenties. He had no great wealth or reputation. He was no great scholar. He held no governmental position. He was only a servant. As such, he was accustomed to being caring rather than cared for. The exposure of the problems of world evangelism were staggering to John Mark. From this fear of the Evangelist we can learn four lessons of the greatest fear of a missionary.

First: SATANIC OPPOSITION! John Mark left the confines of his own country. To leave the confines of one's country and march head-on into the satanic strongholds of this earth can be frightening. The kingdom of darkness is yet unopened by the light of the gospel. But Mark heard the voice of Jesus say, "In My name, in My authority, by My personal presence and power, demonic forces will fall before you. In My name you shall cast out devils. Fear not, timid servant, you go not alone to foreign lands." Jesus said, "When you go, you go with Me, for I will go with you and before you!"

Second: A STRANGE LANGUAGE! Jesus said to Mark, "Fear not: when you and I go together, I will empower you to speak with new tongues." No New Testament reference is ever made to garble or gibberish. Tongues are a known language. Not only does Jesus promise to help missionaries to learn the language, but the promise can even include the miraculous capacity, when necessary, to speak a language that one does not know. God will give to Mark a "strange tongue," one that will embody a heavenly and divinely ordered language. It entails salvation of the world and the individual.

Third: A HOSTILE ENVIRONMENT! Nothing was more devastating to the Evangelist Mark than the shock of the new and different culture. The Apostle Paul and Barnabas had taken Mark into different cultural areas that were unfamiliar to the young missionary. Whenever you are in a different environment, you are bound to have apprehensions and suspicions. In fact, misunderstandings and suspicions abound. But the promise of Jesus is his miraculous protection. For the missionary's need to adjust and survive is undergirded by Jesus' great affirmation: "Lo, I am with you until the end of the ages." Young John Mark's survival in the midst of deadly serpents and their poisonous potions is an assurance of sustenance in the midst of a hostile environment.

Fourth: A RAMPANT DISEASE! What greater fear could this young missionary experience than that of disease—just as for many young missionary couples of today for whom health for themselves and their children is an issue. Jesus' promise of recovery from sickness could include not only physical healing to those who are ministered to on the outside, but to the missionary and his family. Perhaps the greatest wonder of Mark's entire account is whether or not Jesus would use all of the trials and tribulation to authenticate his message to the unbeliever. Sometimes God not only blesses His followers through miraculous healings, He authenticates them through trials and tribulations. The journey may be rough and the hills hard to climb, but when one reaches the mountain and looks back, the unbeliever looks on and sometimes declares the Lord has brought the missionary and his family a mighty long way! We've got a charge to keep!

Finally, in closing, let me share with you an example of how one must go forward in this charge of the Great Commission of our Lord and Savior Jesus Christ. In 1967, on the coldest day recorded on which a professional football game has ever been played, the Green Bay Packers entertained the Dallas Cowboys for the division championship. With less than a minute to play, the Packers were trailing by just two points. The ball was pushed to the Dallas two yard line. At once, the tens of thousands of Green Bay fans stood up and began to cheer: "Charge! Charge! Charge!"

The sportscaster reported that the crowd at this game was the most electrifying, pulsating one they had ever heard. Reverberating, throbbing through the stands were the charging souls of those who awaited the play. The players crouched, with their adrenaline level pumping to the skies, while the quarterback, Bart Starr, called the signal and the center hiked the ball. As one man, the indomitable Packers, driven by the cheer and charge of their fans, pushed the ball across the goal line for the winning touchdown. This charge to go forward has become historic.

Well, there's another "Charge!" It's the charge of Jesus Christ to go forward into all the world and preach his gospel to everyone. Yes, history has recorded many such commissions. Who can forget Patrick Henry's, "Give me liberty or give me death." Who can forget General MacArthur's, "I shall return!" or even Martin Luther King's "I have a dream" speech? But nothing in or out of sacred literature can compare with the last commandment of our Lord, Who said, "Go ye into all the world and preach the Gospel to every creature." The challenge becomes "Have we accepted this charge and will we keep it?"

The Road to Heaven

John 14:6

Richard E. Barnes

In antiquity, the pagan Greeks used a word to describe the disqualified athlete. It is the word *hey'marton*. This word was used to describe a participant who missed sharing in or hitting the mark. If this word was used today, it would apply to a baseball player who, after stepping up to the plate, strikes out. *Hey'marton* translated into our English language is the word for sin! Sin is a description for those who have missed sharing the joy of glorifying the Almighty God while failing to hit the mark, or in plain old baseball language, have struck out because of sin! The great Apostle Paul says in Roman 3:23 that we all have missed sharing in glorifying God. We've all missed the mark. I've struck out and you've struck out and the world continues to strike out!

In the Book of John, Jesus says, "I am the way, the truth, and the life; no man comes to the Father but by me." The word "way" in the Greek is *hodos*, which in the English is the same word for road. This particular road *hodos* has two distinct meanings: one literal and the other metaphorical. However, they cannot be separated one from the other. In the literal sense, a road is the direction one takes to reach his or her destination. In the metaphorical sense, a road suggests one's plans and strategies used to accomplish a particular purpose or goal. Jesus is both the literal and metaphorical road to heaven! He is the road to heaven and has already devised the strategy to get there! Therefore, the only way to deal with sin is to get onto the right road. "Why?" you might be tempted to ask. Well, Jesus is not like us in the sense that He was sinful. He never sinned. Jesus, unlike us, never struck out! He's what we could call in a baseball game the Designated Hitter. He's the Anchor man and the M.V.P. or Most Valuable Player in the game of life. Jesus came to bat for us, the church, and when He stepped to the plate of temptation, He didn't hit a foul ball by allowing Satan to walk with Him, and so Jesus made no errors in this game of life! When our Lord and Savior, Jesus Christ, stepped up to the plate to bat for us as our Designated Hitter, He scored and won the game. He hit a home run straight to heaven and made it possible for all of us to run and make it across home plate. Jesus is the road to heaven!

Unfortunately, many people have lost their souls because they've gotten in the wrong game in this arena called life! They've gotten on the wrong road. You see, you can't get on the road with Buddha and get to heaven. You can't get on the road with the Hindu god Shiva and expect to make it to heaven. You can't walk the road of Hare Krishna and end up in heaven. You can't even walk the road of Islam and make heaven your home. These are not the way, the truth, or the life! Solomon, the son of David and king of Israel, had this to say in Proverbs 14:12: "There is a way or road that seems right unto man, but the end thereof are the ways of death." I remember hearing a story that illustrates the point:

There was a man who enlisted in the Army. He found military life extremely difficult and wanted to get out. Each day he would run around the base searching through trash cans while throwing the papers up after examining each piece of paper. He would then continue shouting, "That's not it! That's not it!" The sergeant noticed his behavior and took him to the CO or commanding officer. Just as soon as the sergeant brought the man in, the man rushed to the trash can and dumped all the papers out, shouting as before, "That's not it! That's not it!" The CO instructed the sergeant to "take this man to the psychologist, who is also the chaplain, and ask him to get to the bottom of this." When they arrived at the psychologist's office, the man repeated this same bizarre action and immediately shouted, "That's not it! That's not it!" and the papers were strewn about over all the floor. Finally, he was given a medical discharge and as he walked toward the gate with his best friend, this friend asked him, "Hey man, what was wrong with you running around shouting, "That's not it!" His friend then asked,

"What were you looking for?" The man held up his discharge papers and said, "This." The friend said, "Oh, I see." The man said, "That's it!"

People are living without homes and dying in despair. Many are seeking peace and tranquility in the worship of Buddha and finding out like the man in the story, "That's not it!" Thousands seek eternal life past and future through Shiva, but "That's not it!" Countless others attribute their good Karma, which is nothing more than the laws of reaping and sowing, to Krishna, but "That's not it!" Many are committed to Islam because they believe that it's the last word from God. Again, I say, "That's not it!" Jesus is still the way, the truth, and the life, and "That's it!" You can't just follow any old body of theology of today!

There's another story of a man who was late getting home for dinner. So, he decided to take a short cut through the graveyard. In his rush to get through the graveyard, he quickly tripped and hit his head on something in the dark. He flicked his lighter to see what it was and discovered it was a tombstone. As the flames danced in the wind, he read the inscription written on the stone: "Stop, my friend, as you walk by. As you are now so once was I. As I am now you soon will be. So come, my friend, and follow me." The man shook his head while reaching into his pocket for a piece of chalk, and he then carved into the stone his response: "To follow you, I'll not consent until I know which way you went!"

You just don't follow people because it seems right or without really knowing where they're going! You've got to get on the right *hodos* or road! And Jesus says: "I am the way!"

Men and women who remained faithful to God have died on this road. Its first martyr was Abel. His father was Adam, who put us all on the wrong road called sin. We sought after a savior who could save us from sin, death, the grave, and an eternal damnation called "hell." Abel gave God the best of the best, and for this his jealous brother took his life. We need to realize that when you give God your best, you're going to attract the devil's attention as well. Satan doesn't want you setting the right example on the road of life because others will see it and imitate your actions. But the devil can't hurt you if you stay on the Lord's road. Enoch walked with God on his road to heaven and the conversation got so good that he literally got carried away.

The road to heaven ran straight up Noah's driveway. God didn't give him the plans to build a Harley Davidson motorcycle, a Lincoln Town Car, or even a speed boat. No, God gave him the plans to build an ark, a kind of cabin cruiser, an ocean liner (Genesis 6:8). Noah found grace in the eyes of the Lord. On the road to heaven, God will give you something to build! And He expects a paramount work from a peculiar people. On the road to heaven we have people's lives to secure by placing them, too, on the road to heaven.

The road to heaven ran straight through Abraham's neighborhood in Genesis 12. It was the road leading out of town which led to a great friendship between Abraham and God. It became the road to a legacy of promise, the promise symbolized in the birth of his son, Isaac. Peter said in Acts 2:38: "Repent and be baptized every one of you in the name of Jesus Christ for the remission of your sins and you shall receive the Gift of the Holy Spirit, for the promise is unto you and your children."

When you travel this road to heaven, you'll need a friend, and not just any old friend will do. However, the song writer expressed it in this way: "What a Friend we have Jesus." Psalms 33:4 says that you can trust in His promises: "For the word of the Lord is right and all His works are done in truth." On the road to heaven, sometimes you can't see clearly, and you'll need to put your trust in God through Christ. The Psalmist says, "Thy word is a lamp unto my feet and a light unto my path." Sometimes when you try to look ahead, it's totally dark. You try to look from side to side and there is nothing there. That's when you have got to plant your feet firmly on the road to heaven and walk worthy of the vocation wherein you are called—trusting in the Lord.

Abraham trusted the Lord when the road led him up to Mt. Moriah, and he found himself there with a knife in his hand. He was obeying his heart and trusting deep within his soul. Isaac remarked, "Father, I see the wood, the knife, and the fire, but where is the sacrifice?" Now, the act of using that knife was just a matter of raising his hand up and down. But Abraham placed his faith right between the up and down of the knife. He knew that God was going to do something; however, he didn't know when, and it could have been after the down direction of the knife. Abraham placed his faith right between the "ups and downs" of God. Parenthetically, let me tell you that God does provide between the "ups and downs" of life. But the key is we must be prepared to make the sacrifices in life. God provided a ram in the bush. And thank God for the "ram" on the road to heaven! When you're traveling the road of life, it's not about the Ohio Lottery, your job, or your family inheritance. You just stay on the road of heaven. Isaac became old and blind; yet, he could still see his way down the road. He knew the personal way who is God! Later on the road, his son Jacob and Jacob's son Joseph and then on to Moses, that Great Emancipator!

The road to heaven carried Moses down the Nile River into the house of Pharaoh, through the back door of the desert, up the mountain, to a burning bush, and back down to the front door of the palace where God rolled out the red carpet of freedom. Moses walked God's people to freedom's land. God detoured his road for a moment and directed him through the Red Sea to give both Moses and us a spiritual lesson. It's to let us know that when our backs are up against the wall and it appears as if we have no place to go, Moses' God will deliver us. When enemies pursue us and friends persecute us, then God will uphold us!

As we walk this road to heaven, we must remember that sin is scattered all along the roadside. We've got to watch out for sin because it will attempt to change our direction. It will make us wander into places that will lead us to devastation. Someone said:

Sin takes you further than you want to go.

Sin costs you more than you want to pay.

Sin keeps you longer than you want to stay.

Watch your travels!

Like David, you're going to have to face some Giants of Goliath!

Like Daniel, you're going to find yourself in dens of lions!

Like the Three Hebrew Boys, you may end up in fiery furnaces!

Like Isaiah, folks will try to cut you in two pieces!

Like John the Baptist, folks will try to make you lose your head!

Like Jesus, you may end up on a cross!

However, never forget that the key to walking this road to heaven is prayer. Prayer is the key to the Kingdom, and faith unlocks the door. Prayer can ease the pain, increase your "can," decrease your strain, and help you maintain! When you learn how to pray, you'll be able to sing the song along the road:

I want Jesus to walk with me,

All along this tedious journey,

I want Jesus to walk with me!

he Problem of Serving Two Masters

Matthew 6:24

C. Jay Matthews

Let me ask you a series of questions: How many of you will agree that God owns the cattle on a thousand hills? How many of you will agree that the earth is the Lord's and the fullness thereof? How many of you will agree that God owns everything? How many of you are God's children? Then, how many of those cattle do you own? How many of you are riding in something that looks like your heavenly Father owns everything? Or, living in some place that looks like you come from a rich family? Or, how many of you have something in your pocket right now that would reflect an inheritance from your divine Father?

If you are missing your portion of your heavenly Father's wealth, it's not because you have been left out of His inheritance. It's probably because you are unaware of the idea of economic empowerment according to divine inheritance. This belongs to you as a result of being a child of God and living in God's world-house. The wealth that I am speaking of goes beyond breathing and the intake of oxygen. It's more than receiving His sunshine in the morning. It extends beyond the "stuff" that He allows to rain upon us!

Should the truth be told, most of us are seldom satisfied! Most of us would want more. If someone gives us a dollar, we could refuse it. However, if someone offers us a million dollars, we would want to know whether there are some strings attached. Well, there are strings attached only when we are attached to God. He is no respecter of persons, and he will give us abundantly and above all that we ask or think! I once asked God, if in fact He owns all of this wealth, then what's wrong with our people? I noticed how other nationalities and ethnic groups are prospering and doing well. I then asked Him, "What do you have against our people?" And he responded, "Nothing, they just need to know the key to economic empowerment."

"No man can serve two masters." The man to whom the text referred is more than an individual. This term can also refer to humanity or mankind. It suggests that the reason why most of us don't have access to God's wealth is because of sin. Too often we have served more than one master—and tried to do so at the same time. Many of us spend most of our lives torn between serving God and serving self. We've jumped right over the devil, and self has become our master. We sit on the throne in our lives. God has already warned us in His word that He is a jealous God. God has informed us that He is not going to share His throne or glory with anybody. However, we constantly perpetuate self. We allow self to rule, will, and conquer. We've developed self-philosophies and self-lifestyles until we've left God out of self!

Others of us have multiple relationships that exclude God. We are too often hooked up with the wrong person. Therefore, we have no fidelity with God. We're in other romances. We go to the church to sing, shout, dance, speak in tongues, prophesy, and a whole gamut of other things. But the bottom line is we too often act like infidels. We talk about loving God while we hold other folk up as gods. These could be your husband, wife, children, or friends. And again, one of the biggest gods is "self." We need to transform our minds and attitude to be more inclusive of God. It is then that we will have access to the wealth of God. Because a person can't serve two masters!

Then the Bible says, **"For either he will hate the one, and love the other."** There's never a comfortable time when we're torn between two relationships whereby one of them does not bother us. They will challenge us with regard to our degree of real affinity. Two relationships are never the same, and one of them will always suffer over the other. Furthermore, the moment one crosses the line and enters into two relationships, commitment is lacking. Often we think we are fully satisfying both relationships, but the devil has blinded us, and one of them will go lacking.

God has been dissatisfied, according to the text, and this places us outside of the blessing of God. Hence, either God is our Lord or something else is lord. God must totally occupy the throne of who we are, and no one else, or He sees this relationship lacking. **"Or else he will hold to the one, and despise the other."**

There are times when we're trying to do what God says in shunning the world and we become angry. It's generally because we are trying to figure out how to make a dual commitment with God and the world. Well, the Bible adds in the text, **"Ye cannot serve God and mammon."** If we replace the word "mammon" with the concept of money, it would read: "Ye cannot serve God and money, possessions, or earthly goods." Too often we spend all our time trying to work for mammon or money! We work most of our hours trying to figure out how to get more, and in the process we are serving mammon. God says you can't serve both. That's a phenomenal idea! Yet, it's more than phenomenal; it's the truth!

In verse 33 of the same text, God suggests the key to economic empowerment: **"But seek ye first the kingdom of God, and his righteousness; and all these things shall be added to you."** We spend our whole life trying to figure out how to get rich but also how to survive. We work all week just to survive! Some of us play the lottery trying to get rich. However, according to Matthew 6:33, our survival and richness are based upon our relationship with God and seeking after righteousness. In the text, God says not only will He help you survive but will add "all of these things"; in Deuteronomy 8:18, "But thou shalt remember. For it is He that giveth thee power to get wealth, that He may establish His covenant which He swore unto thy fathers, as it is this day." So, God gives us the power to get wealth. Too many Christians are conditioned by this American society and a slave mentality to mention the word "wealth." And we ought not to be afraid to collect on God's promises. God promises us that not only will He sustain us from paycheck to paycheck, but also that He will give us vast money or wealth. We are heirs of God and joint heirs with Jesus Christ!

Now the only thing that keeps us from prosperity is the sin nature. Paul suggests this very pointedly in Roman 7:14-20. These verses suggest that the blessings of God will be withdrawn from us if sin is present. When we serve two masters we have sinned. For example, during the Christmas season we are dis-empowered because of the sin issue. Instead of realizing that "Jesus is the reason for the season," we are programmed to give a gift to everyone other than the birthday boy, Jesus! I am sad to report that America is based on greed, individualism, and self. Christian theology is based on Christ. Too many are serving mammon or money instead of God. But when we come into the kingdom, we can also come into wealth!

Our God is a big God! He's big enough that when He said "rain" during Noah's time, it rained long enough to wash away everything but the boat of Noah. He's big enough to save the three Hebrew boys from a fiery furnace. He's big enough to step in a lion's den for Daniel and make them lie down like lambs. He's big enough to declare to all of his children, "I'll bless you in your going out and I'll bless you in your coming in" (Duet. 28). He's big enough to turn things around for us. Hallelujah! We serve a big God! He's too big to let us lie down in debt and not pick us up out of our debts. He's too big to let us drown in debt or leave us outdoors. God is a big God! So high that you can't get over Him. He's so wide that you can't get around Him. He's a real big God! He's so big that when they laid His son, Jesus, in an air-tight, rock-blocked, dark dungeon of a grave, that grave, while locked tight and guarded right, could not hold him. The old preacher of days gone by would exuberantly shout, "Early Sunday morning, Jesus got up out of the grave with all power in His hands!"

Perhaps you are reading this sermon, and you don't know Him or know our big God. Well, He wants you to know him because He wants to make you a "King's kid," a "Child of the kingdom," and a "Guardian of His inheritance."   He wants to meet you. He wants to show you who He is and become the center of your life. He wants to share His love for you. He wants to make you rich in faith and grace. You have a great inheritance waiting for you. The only thing that you need to know is that you don't know Him in your life. You've experienced poverty of life and you want to become rich! He'll make you rich in faith and then add "all these other things unto you." Confess your sins and believe in your heart that God has raised Him from the dead, and you will be saved. You will then be on your road to prosperity! God bless you.

9

The Truth Is the Light

I John 1:5

Timothy M. James

John, the beloved disciple, wrote to the church, in which dissension had arisen and false teachers and false ideas had invaded. Instead of the folk having a breakthrough in their lives, they had broken away from the church. The dissension settled on the denials of the false teachers around the doctrine of Christ. They denied that Jesus was the Christ. They denied that Jesus came from God. They denied the authority of Jesus' commands and their own sinfulness. They went as far as to deny salvation through the saving grace of Jesus Christ. Finally, they denied the demand and the commandment that Christians should love one another. To all these denials and to the conflicts in the church, John writes, through the inspiration of the Holy Spirit, to simply encourage the people and the church to live in God's light.

John's message to the church is the same today as it was during the early church existence. It centers on the life and teachings of Jesus Christ. John is passing it on to us. This is not a second-hand twisted gossip; this is first-hand information based on an eye-witness account. It is from a heart that was changed by Jesus Christ, the Son of God!

There are many who would like to receive the crown of eternal life. They would like to receive it without carrying the cross of obedience, sacrifice, and love. A man's character is determined by the very god he serves. That is why John lays out for us the nature of God, the Father of our Lord Jesus Christ. It is He whom we serve in order that His nature may be seen in us. John says, "God is light and there is no darkness in Him." William Barclay described the characteristics of God's light as:

Splendor and glory; wonderful, ablaze piercing in the darkness. Self-revealing, light is seen, brightening things around it. God is not a secret; He wants to be seen and known by men. Light tells us of God's purity and holiness. There is nothing dark about Him. He has nothing to hide. In Him is no evil. He is purity and stainless holiness. Light tells us God is our guide; light shows us the way. He offers guidance for our footsteps; a light and a lamp. Light is the revealing quality of the presence of God. In His presence all of our blemishes are realized and obvious; our imperfections and filth and flaws are brought to the light in His presence. Thus, Isaiah cried, "I am undone, I am a man of unclean lips, I was born and shaped in iniquity." We never know how low we have fallen or how lofty we have risen until we see it in the revealing light of the presence of God.[1]

THE TRUTH IS THE LIGHT!

In God there is no darkness! This darkness of which I speak is not about color. It is not about skin tone of a curse. Black is beautiful. The color of Africans and descendants of Africans all over the world is not the color of a curse. Even God's own Son bore this skin color, for the Bible says: "Out of Africa have I called my Son" (Hosea 11:1).[2]

This darkness is the opposite of God and therefore the opposite of the Christian life. William Barclay further tells us about this darkness when he affirms, "A Christian life, unlike the man before he met the Lord, or the man who strays away from Him." John says, "Those who follow Christ shall not walk in darkness, as others do, but have the light of life." The Apostle Peter adds, "God has called me out of the darkness into His marvelous light." The hostility of darkness is that it tries to overcome the light. The dark and the light are natural enemies. John begins his Gospel by saying that the light that God gave shines in the darkness, and the darkness shall not overcome it! The darkness is the ignorance of a life apart from Christ. Without Christ we are lost in the darkness of sin and do not

1. William Barclay, *The Letters of John and Jude* (Philadelphia: Westminster Press, 1976).
2. Cain Hope Felder, *The Original African Heritage Study Bible* (Nashville: Winston & Derek, 1993).

know which way to go. The darkness represents the chaos of life without Christ. Look back, if you will, to the first act of creation. God commanded the light to shine out of the darkness. Without God's light this becomes a chaotic world, void of order or sense. This darkness is the immorality in the lives of those who don't know Christ. These are deeds of darkness; they are not like Christ. Such persons seek the shadows, the shade, and the darkness of night to do their evil things. Such persons cannot stand the light.

Darkness is unfruitful. Those who work in darkness work toward pleasure and temporary praise. It is not long-lasting because, like plants that grow in darkness, it will neither grow nor produce fruit. Neither will the spirit of man reach the Spirit of God in darkness. Darkness stands for loneliness and hurt, and all around the world and in the home there is the darkness of loneliness.

Finally, darkness is the devil's backyard. It is the abode and habitat of the enemies of God. It is the destination and the goal of those who will not accept Jesus Christ as Savior and Lord. It is a struggle for Christ and the Christians against the rulers of darkness. It is essential that we walk in the light. THE TRUTH IS THE LIGHT!

We ought not to "fool" ourselves but rather "prove" ourselves. We can know whether we're walking in the light. Some thought their spiritual knowledge, their worship practices, and their sacrifices made them repellent to sin! They thought they could not be stained by sin no matter what they did. But God declares all unrighteousness is sin. But as the people of God and the Church of God, we are to believe in the God of pure goodness and to become like Him! Leviticus declares: "You shall be holy; for I the Lord your God am holy." Hence, our fellowship with God draws us closer to Him, and sin becomes the more terrible to us. We ought not just to know the truth, but do it! Christian truth is not only intellectual, it is always moral. It is obedience to His word and commands. The intellectual problem will result in arrogance and pride. For the Christian, truth is something first to be discovered and then obeyed. THE TRUTH IS THE LIGHT!

When you walk in the light, you have fellowship one with the other. Psalms 133 reads, "Behold, how good and how pleasant it is for brethren to dwell together in unity!" Consequently, Christianity is not merely a solitary religion. It is a united religion with the goal of unity, togetherness, and harmony. Hence, no local church can be exclusively unto itself, for anything that destroys fellowship cannot be the true church.

In truth, we are daily cleansed more and more from sin by the precious blood of Jesus. Day by day, one day at a time, step by step, we are being cleansed. John affirms in our very being that, if we really know the sacrifice of God in Christ, things will be different. If, in fact, we have had a real experience of His power, then day by day we will have holiness in our lives. We will become more fit to enter into His presence. The blood that Jesus shed cleanses us from all sin; our past sins are removed, and we are strengthened and equipped for holiness. This holiness is exhibited on a day-to-day basis. Therefore, true religion is a daily religion. It's the kind of religion that causes us to grow closer in fellowship one with the other. This kind of fellowship will lead to a genuine fellowship with God. We then will have fellowship with man and God or God and man. These lead us to both a horizontal and vertical relationship that makes us complete in the cross. THE TRUTH IS THE LIGHT! God is light and we must walk in the light. He is a marvelous light! He is a glorious light! He is a revealing light! He is a guiding light! He is a radiant light! He is a cleansing light! He is a saving light! He is a loving light!

We'll walk in the light, beautiful light,

Come where the dew drops of mercy shine bright.

Shine all around us by day and by night,

Jesus the light of the world. Amen.

(From "Jesus the Light of the World";
words by George D. Elderkin)

Satanic Breakthrough!

Job 1:1-12

Larry Lawrence Harris

Here in the text we find Job in a sovereign setup and unaware of an imminent Satanic breakthrough. Calamity riding on the chariot of Satanic devastation is only days away from capsizing the life of Job! Yet, it is necessary to keep in mind that Satan did not initiate this breakthrough. No, it was God! The almighty God Himself chose Job for this divine setup by this satanic breakthrough. It was God who summoned the angelic world before Him. It was God who said to Satan, "Have you considered my servant Job?" It was God who superimposed the exaltation of Job on the mind of Satan. And in verse 8, God said, "There is none like him in the land." In other words, God informed Satan that Job was perfect or spiritually mature. Job was upright or had right standing with the Lord. Job was God fearing, which means he held God in the highest of respect and reverence. Furthermore, Job eschewed evils and was always avoiding sin in his life or community.

Thus, it was God who bragged about Job and asked, "Have you considered my servant Job?" This suggests to me that sometimes God brags about us! When we are in His will and following His commands, when we attempt to do the right thing and refrain from doing evil, God brags about us!

If you will allow me, I'd like to look at the tenth verse and draw closer to it because it is in this verse that we find Satan giving his rebuttal to God Almighty. Satan responds to God's accolades of Job by saying the only reason Job serves Him is because God has built a hedge around him. The assertion is that God had a hedge around all of Job's possessions and had blessed the work of his hands to the point that there was an increase in his stock. In other words, the allegation is Job was serving God for what he could get out of God. And so, Satan says in verse 11 that if Job received a crushing blow to his material possessions and was stripped of everything, Job would curse God to His face. This argument was Satan's voucher for a breakthrough on the life of Job. But wait a minute! This argument serves notice on all of us that Satan desires to break through the walls of our possession and protection. Therefore, it is the will of Satan to harm and hinder us before we leave this earth.

Let us consider Job's response and gain some needful insights as to how to handle a satanic breakthrough! To this, let us consider four points: (1) the Requisition granted to Satan by God; (2) the Request that devastates Job's world; (3) the Response to satanic breakthrough; and (4) the Rebounding Man.

Requisition Granted

In verse 11 God gives Satan, the accuser, permission to "put forth thine hand and touch all that he hath...and Job will curse you." In verse 12, God, Job's advocate, says, "All that he has is in your power; only do not touch him physically." Hence, God grants Satan's request. The question becomes, why? Well, I believe in order to answer some of life's deep questions, God sometimes grants Satan's requests. These are times in which Christian living asks such questions as: Will we serve God if there are no personal gains? Are we using worship as a coin to purchase heavenly favors and rewards? Is piety a contract by which we gain wealth and ward off trouble?

I believe God grants Satan's requests at times to show us how limited Satan really is in the midst of a powerful God! Sometimes Satan is granted permission to harm us so that we can realize that God has not left us. It will remind us that God knows how much we can bear. We will then learn the lesson, that God does place limits on Satan's attacks in time and eternity. There are times in which God must teach us His sovereignty through a contrast of the power of God and Satan's subservient power. We must be reminded that Satan is limited and he is not omnipotent, omniscient, or omnipresent!

In the story, Satan thought if God removed the hedge of blessings from around Job's life then Job would curse God. God granted the request of Satan. Initially, Job did not know why, because God didn't tell him. But Job's faith was challenged to believe that God knows best!

Request That Devastates

In the story, Satan immediately and unrelentingly tears down the hedge in the life of Job. The hedge which stood for a boundary, a barrier, a limit, and a means of protection—the hedge which stood for the blessings of God both visible and invisible. Satan then concentrates on Job's possessions and earthly goods. He moves from that point of devastation to the physical destruction of his family. Job's sons and daughters are destroyed by an east wind. His personal health deteriorates and he suffers physical loss. Job's hedge of relationship with God is challenged. His right standing with God and reverence, respect, and love for God are at risk.

The Bible says in verses 14-19 that "while he was yet speaking" several crushing blows occur that are sent by Satan against the life of Job. However, another set of phrases occurs simultaneously: "I only am escaped to tell thee." This statement serves as a period and an exclamation point to bring a close to certain statements of joy once held in the life of Job. These statements combined to speak of a total wipe-out of the once prosperous Job in the land of Uz. Therefore, in one day Job lost his wealth, family, and health! Such statements ought to remind us that in life we ought not to hold the possessions of life too closely. We need to be reminded through such storms of life that we are only the stewards, not the owners, of our possessions.

Response of Job

How does Job handle this satanic response? Well, we must remember that Job is a special man of God. He is a part of the family of God and not of this world. Job does have faults and failures, imperfections and inadequacies, but he is nevertheless God's child! Therefore, Job acts accordingly as a real man. He openly displays his emotions and is grieved. He tears his clothes and shaves his head. Job realizes that he is in mourning. He must mourn the loss of his family, fortune, and fame. But Job is also a righteous man, and in verse 20 he gives God His praise. Outwardly, Job expresses his trust in God in spite of his storm and difficulty. And Job knew all that he had belonged to God. So he says, "Naked came I, naked shall I return" (verse 21). Job remembers that it was the Lord who dressed him with clothing. He reminds himself of the supplier of basic needs such as food and shelter. He affirms God as the giver of family, friends, and foes. He is aware that the Lord will one day undress him and take everything away, be they family, fortune, or friends.

A Rebounding Man

Job concludes in verse 21, "Blessed be the name of the Lord!" Like the Psalmist who wrote the 103rd Psalm, Job blessed the Lord. He rises up and refuses to stay down. The Bible suggests that he got up! The question for us to ask is: What will we do when God allows Satan's breakthrough in our life? Will we attempt to fight Satan in our own might? If so, we will soon discover we've endeavored in a losing battle. When God allows a Satanic breakthrough, will we run to our peers? Will we find a bottle of drugs or alcohol? Or, will we run to our hiding places? Job gives us the answer when he decides to run to God. Ephesians 6:12-13 says:

> Put on the whole armour of God, that ye may be able to stand against the wiles of the devil. For we wrestle not against principalities, against powers, against the rulers of the darkness of this world, against spiritual wickedness in high places. Wherefore, take unto you the whole armour of God, that ye may be able to withstand in the evil day, and having done all, stand.

Standing on the Rock

Psalms 11:13

Henry James Payden, Sr.

Someone has suggested that the world in which we live has become a madhouse with the inmates trying to run the asylum. These are evil times where all kinds of tricks are being played on people. Today, I speak to you as an individual. I am not chiming in with any group or marching in the sway of any movement. This is a solitary voice. But I'm tired of what's going on in our world today! I can speak today because I am an American by birth, a Christian by the second birth, and a Baptist by conviction. I am not interested in theological fads that change as quickly as youthful fads. I am not among the spiritual adolescents and the immature who are tossed about with every wind of doctrine. Therefore, I do have a voice!

There are a few things that I am tired of, and I need to bring them to your attention! I'm tired of hearing how our denominations should get away from their humble beginnings and "shake the hayseed out of their hair and come of age." I'm tired of all these modern efforts to force a counterfeit kingdom of heaven upon an unregenerate society. That's the kind of theology that will only sweep out one devil so that seven may return. I'm tired of the church speaking softly on the immoralities of our times. They are only making moral issues into political projects. Therefore, I'm tired of "experts" who know all the answers while yet to find out what ought to have been the question. I'm tired of this joke called progress which is no more than regress and failure. We've learned how to lengthen life and not to deepen it! Our foreparents held on to deep living. They could do more with one dollar than we can do with one hundred dollars. With no schooling, they knew more about counting than we who have graduate degrees. They did more with

less! Our foreparents could tell us more about the Christ in their
life and knew how to testify about His blessings. Yet, most of us
complain about the blessings we don't have!

I'm tired of many more things! I'm tired of the stupidity of
our smartness. Look at us, in this modern technological age. We
cut down the trees that God placed for oxidation. We've polluted
the waters and rivers and turned them into sewers. Lung and throat
cancer are prevalent today, and yet we still won't stop smoking. Our
cities have become a jungle of crime where decent women are afraid
to walk our streets. We are living in a madhouse of noise and of ear-
splitting, traffic roaring, rock and rolling, transistorizing radios. We
have jet airliners overhead and power mowers around us. Our teen-
age youth are screeching through the streets with their bee-bop
music, and demonstrators are marching for their so-called rights!
And in desperation we move to the country, build us a cottage, and
then wake up one morning only to find bulldozers clearing away
everything around us to make a highway at our front doors. I tell
you, I'm tired!

We live in a strange world. It's far different from the one I
knew. It's a world where you don't need a name, or the name of your
father or mother anymore. We live by a social security number, an
American Express card, a Visa card, and a Master Charge. We are
tagged, labeled, and cataloged according to the mark of the beast.
I tell you we are messed up! We're messed up in our theology.
Many of our people read these demonic commentaries that deny the
virgin birth and say that miracles are something of the past. Instead
of calling immorality sin, we say that such a person has a sickness.

Must I go on? Why should I go on about the things that have
made me tired? Let me focus on what man can believe for certain.
Josh Billings said some years ago, "I'd rather know a few things for
certain than to be sure of a lot things that are not so!" There are
seven things that I am certain about for those of you, like me, who
are tired!

1. **I believe the Bible is the Word of God (Good News)!**
    There is no "if" or "but," "possibly," or "maybe"; the Bi-
    ble is God's word! Listen to me, who does not boast of
    being a "Protestant" but a "Proclaimer. I'm not told by
    God to "explain," just to "proclaim." I must admit that I
    don't understand it all, but I can stand on His Word! The
    Word of God needs no vindication. It's not to be argued.
    The Bible has been buried many times and even now men

would try to bury God Himself, if possible.   However, this "corpse" has a way of coming to life in the midst of interment where the pallbearers have already lined up! The Bible is not a myth; it's a miracle! And the Bible is the solid Rock upon which I stand!

2. **I believe that Jesus Christ is the Son of God!** He was born of the Virgin Mary. Otherwise, He would have been born out of wedlock, and I'm not interested in that kind of Savior. John 3:16 says, "For God so loved the world that He gave His only begotten so that whosoever believeth in Him should not perish but have everlasting life." He's the solid Rock I stand upon!

3. **I believe that Jesus Christ died for our sins!** Jesus did not only come to teach us some exemplary lessons. He didn't come to merely become an example for us to follow. He did not die a mere martyr's death. But, He came to do something about our main problem called "sin." When we sin, we ought not to run from Jesus, but to Him. He forgives! Jesus died on the cross for our sins. He came to save us and deliver us. He is the foundation and Rock I stand upon!

4. **I believe that Jesus rose bodily from the grave!** The resurrection of Jesus Christ is the world's greatest secret. The church is the greatest secret order of all times. But the secret of the resurrection has been revealed to the world in the Gospels' accounts. I accept his resurrection. The world knows He died and the church knows He arose. I live in the power and experience of His resurrection. A song writer once wrote, "Up from the grave He arose."

5. **I believe that Jesus is coming back personally to reign and rule the earth!** It could be any day! The sooner will be the better. Man is an unholy mess and only Jesus can bring him out of the mess. When Jesus came the first time, neither Grecian, Roman, nor Jew would receive Him. When Jesus comes again to the earth, neither government, culture, nor religion will hang out a "Welcome" sign. Even the church is so busy puttering around that she scarcely lifts her eyes heavenward to pray. "Even so, come Lord Jesus." Wouldn't you think that this subject of Christ's second coming would be on all of our lips? It

ought to be the topic of many a happy Christian. Try to bring up the subject and then watch the suspicious, hesitant faces of the most embarrassed. Why? Because the Lord's return is the unwanted stepchild in the family of church doctrine.

6.   **I believe that the true church is the good society of all people who have been twice born!** The true church to which I refer is not the ecclesiastical octopus or the world church which has been shaped by Herbert Armstrong. Armstrong thinks that the church will end under the rulership and dominion of the anti-christ. When I speak of the true church, I'm not talking about the fictitious bishops who have confused preachers. Too many of our preachers are acrobatic preachers who have produced circus congregations. They only shout while the music is playing. However, only the true church will be officially recognized in that day when the Lord returns. The true church, where the statistics are in heaven, that fellowships in the Spirit, whose foundation is in Jesus Christ, will stand! It is not the true church because she speaks in tongues or because she's taught how to do the holy dance. She is the true church because she has been washed in the blood of the Lamb!

7.   **I believe in Heaven!** Heaven is our home. It's the believer's place of joy, bliss, comfort, and healing! My Savior is there. The Word of God tells me so. "In my Father's house are many mansions. I go to prepare a place for you that where I am, you may be also" (John 14:1). Jesus is in heaven and I'll one day join Him there. That settles it. If it were not true then He would have told us. God said it! I believe it! And that settles it! But whether I believe it or not, God said it and that settles it! I can take God's word as truth because in His being who He is, I'm told that God cannot lie! For all that He is, I take Him. For all that I need, I trust Him. For every blessing, I thank Him. For all who trust Him will have eternal life. For all who reject Him will live in torment or eternal damnation. I'm going to stand on the Rock of my salvation!

No Risks, No Rewards

Acts 8:26-40

William H. Myers

The story of the Ethiopian finance minister invades the mind of the modern reader with a lot of questions. What is an angel, an Ethiopian, a eunuch in this context? What is and who was Candace? Even scholars wrestle with points of exegetical significance and insignificance. Should we translate "southward" or "at noon," desert or desert city? Was the Ethiopian immersed in the water or not? Was he reading a Greek or Hebrew text?

What I find striking in this text, however, are the radical twists and the intriguing risks that emerge in the story. These elements are as varied as the exegetical points that are vigorously debated. I can touch on only a few.

Where are the apostles? Luke juxtaposes the twelve and the seven earlier in a way that leaves one with the impression that the twelve are the first string in Pauline terms, the foundation of the church, and the seven are the second string in Lukan terms. Are they table waiters or helpers of those on the first team? In certain parts of the Church today, that view still prevails. Yet, just as soon as Luke appears to establish such a dogma, he immediately shatters it with a series of narratives that shed some light on praxis as it really existed. In these narratives, including the present one, the second team fulfills a role the reader was set up to believe was relegated to the first team.

Wasn't it the apostles, the first squad, that Jesus commanded to carry the gospel to Jerusalem, Judea, Samaria, and the ends of the earth? However, in light of Luke's description—that all were scattered throughout the various regions and those who were scattered went about preaching the word, except the apostles— one can't help but raise a series of questions. For example, did the first team's ethnic bias get in their way and limit, at least initially, what they otherwise could have accomplished?

The apostles were granted the mountain and lake experiences with Jesus, the advantage of insider data and private discussions, and the secret sharing and exchange of information among this somewhat tightly held brotherhood. They had open and unobstructed access to the knowledge of the Word. It is noteworthy, then, to observe how they resisted allowing certain groups access to this same information to which they were privy. It appears that only a direct confrontation by God with Peter, their leader, could loose them from their prejudices long enough to widen the circle. It took a series of significant events to make clear God's activity to, for, and with other ethnic groups, without the first team's help to exorcise that demon within them.

Then, there is the matter of communication from an angel of the Lord and the Spirit of the Lord. The latter is a little less troublesome for most, but the former creates all kind of problems. It's tough enough in modern times getting anyone to believe that the Spirit of the Lord led you to do anything, let alone declaring that you received a message from an angel. You probably won't even get the opportunity to inform the listener whether the angel appeared in human form or some other, with or without wings, whether it was draped in a white robe and kinte cloth or street clothes, before the men in white suits and kinte cloth arrive. Such claims could get you locked up.

However one comes out on this matter—whether a literal angel or supernatural guidance—does not diminish the radical risk of the communication, because there still remains a significant amount of ambiguity even after the divine has spoken. This is indeed radical and risky, because one would normally expect that if there is one form of communication in this universe that should be clear, it is a message from the divine. Isn't that what a large part of the church today believes? When God speaks there is absolute clarity, no ambiguity.

On the contrary. Such is the nature of the call. Such is the whisper of God, the encounter with angels, the command of the Spirit. You can only hear it with an ear of faith. Did you hear it? Did anyone else hear it? Are you sure? What was the message? What does it mean?

Notice the force of the story. Philip has no idea where he is going or why he is going. Just head south on the road that runs from

Jerusalem to Gaza. Where on the road is he supposed to go? That road is approximately eighty miles long. But, the angel of the Lord merely says, just point your face south and start walking. He has no idea what he is supposed to do. Just go south on this very long road. He has no idea who he is supposed to meet, if anybody. Just go south. Worst yet, he is supposed to go at noon along this desert road. Nobody travels at noon in the desert in Palestine, let alone eighty miles. It's too hot. This is a very radical risk.

The man Philip meets is paradoxically radical to the modern reader. He is a financially powerful, multilingual black man who knows and worships God before he meets Philip. In addition, depending on how one chooses to understand the eunuch, this Ethiopian brother may have also carried a legal and social stigma. Moreover, in Luke's literary design, the Ethiopian story, not the Cornelius story, is the first to move the gospel into the Gentile world and fulfill Jesus's command to take the gospel to the ends of the earth, in spite of the lack of acknowledgment of same in the history of interpretation. Now then, in how many books, even in modern times, is a black man also regally depicted?

Two men's lives intersected, one from Palestine, the other from Africa, in an awkward place at an awkward time, and the course of history was altered. The choice of them as servants seems both risky and radical; so too was their mission. It was in the midst of taking the risk that Philip learned just how radical were the conditions that God was calling him to. He knew that God was calling him in general, but he had no idea about the particulars. That is often how God works with us in an effort to determine just how committed we are. Will we take a risk for God merely because we sense the need is there, even when we can't grasp all the particulars at that moment?

Radical conditions call upon a follower of Jesus to be radical in his or her risks for the Lord. That is what faith is all about: stepping out, not when you can see clearly, not when it is safe, not when you have it all mapped out before you, but when you can't see clearly, when it isn't safe, when the fog hangs so low you can't feel your way, when things are so ambiguous that there appears to be no reality, when you don't even know where you are going, or why you are going, or if it makes sense for you to go, or if you are going to make it. All you know is that you are being driven south, ever south into the desert, deep into the desert by the Spirit of the Lord. Your desire might be to go east; you might have even charted your course eastward, but a whisper in the wind says south. Believe me, it's always a whisper because the forces within and the forces without continue to raise questions in your mind about the call to head south. However, you heard it and responded, even though you're not totally sure where you're going or why you're going. It seems to me that's what it really means to be a risk-taker for the Lord.

Five years ago I met with a group of "Ethiopians" in a desert place called Collegevile, Minnesota. It was certainly a historic event. I had never met that many Ethiopian biblical scholars under one roof at the same time. It was truly a desert place: no VCR, no television, no queen-size beds, no Convenient Mart, Winn-Dixie, or Lawsons; nothing but piranha flies and heat, heat on top of heat. The risk was immeasurable. I didn't know any of these people, not really. I had met Tom Hoyt the year before in Anaheim at the Society of Biblical Literature, and he invited me to this gathering. We talked briefly about a need, a need that was close to my heart. He didn't look like any angel that I had ever seen or heard, but I heard a whisper in the wind that said, go north to Collegeville.

Yet, I had no clear sense of where I was going or why I was going or, for that matter, what I was supposed to do when I got there. I didn't even know who I was going to meet when I got there. Worst yet, I didn't even know it was a desert place. What a risk. It soon became evident to me that I was not the only one seeking clarity in this state of ambiguity. It was a bold vision, but oh what a risk. The risks became more evident as the years went by. We wondered if clarity could ever come in the midst of a desert. Could there be any worthy result from such a mission? A desert place does not appear to be the best place to gain understanding and clarity of thought. It's too hot, and sometimes it was hotter than other times.

At times the desert was so foreboding and the risks so radical that it just didn't seem worth it. All of us were involved in so many other things that held at least equal, if not greater, importance to us at that time—things that for the most part did not require negotiation with a dozen or more "Ethiopians." Other realities called into question the sense of this desert experience for some of us. Each person there risked something precious.

The second year, I left the day before the session was complete because I received word that a very close friend's son and daughter had drowned. He was nine years old, and she was eleven. He fell into a pond and couldn't swim, and his sister, who couldn't swim either, jumped in to rescue him and both drowned. Their mother and I grew up as adolescents in church together. My wife was their Sunday school teacher. Their names were frequently mentioned around our house. They were like my own children. The mother was distraught. The father devastated. How could I not go?

The desert experience no longer seemed worth it. It faded as a distant memory on the flight back, as I was enveloped in the silence that tore through to my innermost being—the silence of my colleagues' voices that I left behind, the silence on the plane, the silence within, the silence of those two sweet voices replaying endlessly within. Only my youngest brother's death two years before had cut any deeper into my soul. Never have I seen two more angelic children in my life. What could I say? What would I say? Especially since I knew that the "spiritual speakeasies"—to borrow a phrase from Gardner Taylor's *How Shall They Preach*—would have made their visit before I arrived. What do you say in an event like that that does not either mock God or mock the bereaved? So, I held her in my arms, and I listened as he talked and she talked as long as they wanted to talk, and then I merely sat with them. In the reality of that living room, Collegeville was a flame about to be snuffed.

However, I received letters from many of those Ethiopian colleagues asking me to rejoin the chariot in the desert where understanding was being sought. Again, the whisper in the wind that had never really left me returned, and the flame was reignited. It was not all smooth sailing even as the various essays started to come in. But one reality emerged in the midst of that desert experience: those who heard the voice of the angel and responded decided to stay the course, no matter how stony the road.

Hence, *Stony the Road We Trod* was given birth by some Ethiopian biblical scholars who met in a desert place, took some radical risks, overcame some overwhelming odds, and yielded some radical results. Truly, the road that led to its production was a stony road indeed, for each of us. Like the seven, we were a kind of second squad, not the first squad who had been close to the knowledge of the Word but had refused to share all they knew. Yet, like similar works from Ethiopians of other disciplines, it makes clear how God is at work in our ethnic group as well, and I think in its own small way it will help to alter the course of biblical interpretation in years to come.

I am both humbled and honored at this publication that will take its place in the religious academy. However, for me, in the years to come, every time I see or hear about this work I will always associate it with Andre and Latausha, and thus be reminded what this mission is all about: two little Ethiopians, both of whom went down into the water and when they came up out of the water went back home rejoicing. Hence, my challenge to each of you is framed in a simple question: What risks will this transfiguration experience spur you to take on behalf of other Ethiopians in the desert to which you have been called? No risks, no rewards!

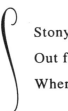

Stony the road we trod, bitter the chastening rod,

Out from the gloomy past, till now we stand at last,

Where the white gleam of our bright star is cast.

Casualties of War

1 Peter 2:11, Ephesians 6:12–17

Andrew Edwards

Casualty is a concept used to describe anyone who is victimized by an accident. It could also refer to one who is harmed or eliminated as a result of an action or circumstance. But, the military use of the word refers to one injured, killed, captured, or missing in action through engagement with an enemy (*The American Heritage Dictionary*, Third Edition, 1992).

Every war has casualties! In every war, there is someone lost or missing in action who will never be found or seen again. Some soldiers are wounded, maimed, left crippled emotionally or physically. Their injury can result in their being categorized as disabled. Also, some people, whether civilian or military status, lose their lives as a result of war. These are all examples of casualties of war.

Very few people are around who were active in World War I. But we do have many mature, aged members who were active in World War II. We have some members who participated in the Korean Conflict and others who were involved in the Vietnam/Southeast Asian War. Now we have some folks who are veterans of that brief military campaign that lasted less than two months, the Persian Gulf War of 1991. The Persian Gulf War was a unique war. It was a war of technology where an African American served as Chairman of the Joint Chiefs of Staff, and a war that gave pride to a nation with a low priority for military concerns. The veterans came home with a sense of pride. But there were still casualties, even in that technological war (Powell, 1995; *Compton's Interactive Encyclopedia*, 1996).

Two social scientists in the early 1970s took a unique approach in their analysis of society in their book entitled *The Triple Revo-*

lution: Emerging Social Problems in Depth. They analyzed (1) Technological Militarism, including social and psychological consequences of nuclear capabilities; (2) Cybernation, including the age of automation and centralization of big business; and (3) Human Rights, the struggle with racism, poverty, and inequality (Perrucci and Pilisuk, 1971). They were illustrating and forecasting how there can be casualties from social revolution or social changes in a complex society. Indeed, there have been devastation, loss of employment, emotional stress, homelessness, and identity conflicts as a result of what they termed the Triple Revolution.

But there is another major war that is often overlooked by our newspapers, electronic media, and most social scientists. That is, The War Against The Soul. This war was started during the time when there were no more than one or two individuals in the world and it is still in process. It is an ongoing conflict that tears at the very core of our being. It is a major conflict that can result in serious wounds. Some individuals are actually captured by the enemy. The conflict may cause the disappearance of some individuals, or even physical or spiritual death. It is a serious conflict. That is why the apostle Peter referred to it as a war. It is a war capable of great devastation. It is a war against the soul.

Theological Significance

This is a war with no retired veterans who take part in parades on Memorial Day. Veterans of this war will have to wait until the next dimension of life (life in eternity with God) before they can truly celebrate victory (John 14:1-3; Revelation 2:10). The faithful soldiers may receive a crown of life.

But like every war, this war produces some casualties. Some are civilians. Little children who are innocent may have their lives cruelly devastated by an evil force that is striking out at God's church, the barracks for various divisions of the army of God. Some families lose a father or a mother because one seemed to be committed but was not strong enough to remain vigilant. Consequently, they were lost in action and may not be seen again by their loved ones. Others have been wounded deeply by illicit drug use and now are emotionally or physically crippled. The enemy uses sophisticated, complex weapons that can be categorized as a kind of biological and chemical warfare. These weapons of mass destruction hurt Christian soldiers as well as civilians on the sidelines who have not enlisted in the army. But the evil one, Satan, actually intends to inflict pain on the civilian population because many people get confused and blame someone other than the real enemy.

Today, we are here to give comfort to those who have lost someone in this great spiritual warfare. Also, we want to encourage our people to grow in their ability to fight the spiritual fight. It was the inspired apostle Paul who wrote, "For we wrestle not against flesh and blood, but against powers, against the rulers of the darkness of this world, against spiritual wickedness in high places" (Ephesians 6:12).

I spent several years in the U.S. Army Reserves. I completed Basic Training and Advanced Individual Training with the regular army personnel preparing for infantry assignments. My drill instructor (drill sergeant) would periodically remind us that his job was to train us so that we would not become casualties of war. He would also remind us and himself that no matter how hard he tried to teach us survival skills and proper military methods, some people would reject his training and become casualties anyway. But if we did become statistics of killed, missing-in-action, or wounded soldiers, it would not be his fault.

We must be as military watchmen who have the awesome responsibility of warning others of the impending dangers that may come in the form of an invasion. If the people heed our warning, then they shall be spared. If the people reject or fail to respond to our warning, then they shall perish. But if we fail to proclaim the danger to the people, and some of them actually do perish, then we shall be held accountable for the loss of their life (Ezekiel 33:1-6). That is a major role of the church. In addition to proclaiming the message of salvation, we must train and equip the committed Christians to put on "...the whole armor of God, that you may be able to withstand in the evil day, and having all, to stand" (Ephesians 6:13).

The Contemporary Challenge

As a church we must be concerned about the "...least of these in our society. Those that are strangers, homeless, hungry, in need of clothing and the sick" (Matt. 25:31–46). They represent casualties of a great spiritual war. Some may represent deserters, others are wounded soldiers, still others are victims who did not know a war was in progress. Too often, our people misunderstand that there is a war and an enemy soldier. The real enemy is not a particular political party. It is not the federal government or any of its multitude of agencies. It is not the educational system. The true enemy is not a particular racial or cultural group, or a social political ideology. The true enemy is Satan, the spirit of darkness. He is a personality and a force that can and will use any group to create destruction in our world. Such destruction can lead to a doubt concerning the reality of love, mercy, grace, and sacrifice that is central to the essence of God.

Without embracing a faith in God and Jesus, as the son of God, redeemer of our soul, then there is no real hope. Thus, the human casualties of the great war against the soul need someone to care for their human wounds. We must show them our faith by our works (James 2:14–20). As soldiers in the Lord's army, we must be as compassionate and committed to one another as contemporary soldiers are to their comrades-in-arms. They are taught to search for, assist, and rescue one another when captured. However, too often the church is the only army that kills its own wounded. As much as we hate the devastation of heroin, cocaine, and other illicit drugs, we must reach out to the drug user as a wounded individual in a great spiritual warfare. As much as we hate bigotry in its many forms, we must reach out to the bigot as one emotionally and mentally wounded by the great spiritual war. As much as we hate violence that destroys our families and community, we must reach out to the perpetrators and try to bring spiritual healing to them. We must have a ministry of reconciliation.

However, we cannot approach the wounded or the enemy's agents without proper protection. We must have our spiritually sensitive parts protected, reinforced, and wrapped with a protective coating of truth, the breastplate of righteousness, the gospel of peace, the shield of faith, and the helmet of salvation. But as a weapon, we need the sword of the Spirit of God (Ephesians 6:14–17).

We are in a war! It is a spiritual war against the soul. A war against a political party could end when a new government is established or the old one reaffirms its ability to rule. A war against a disease could end when a cure has been found and distributed among the people. A war against crime could end when protection of the people with established laws and equal treatment becomes a dominant pattern. But this war is continuous. And in this war there are no forms of "Exemption from Service." Everyone must fight battles in this war. No one can fight it for you! It is a war against the creations of God, who are made for the praise and glory of God. In this war we must fight and resist all kinds of temptations that destroy the soul. It is a war against the soul! Some scholars may debate the meaning of the word psyche (soul) in the passage of I Peter 2:11. Some say that it refers to our spiritual entity, that which will be our everlasting identity in eternity. Others suggest that in this context it refers to our whole self, even our body (Blum 1981). But the central message is that we are in danger from Satan's attack. Satan wishes to attack our body and soul. Therefore, we must fight and resist sexual immorality because it represents **a war against the soul!** We must fight and resist gambling and all forms of greed because those things represent **a war against the soul!** We must fight and resist finding our pleasure in revenge because it represents **a war against the soul!** We must reject the temptation to get high on alcoholic drinks and mind-altering drugs because they represent **a war against the soul!** We must remain firmly rooted in the will of God and depend on the Lord for strength or else we could become a casualty of war! Anything outside of the will of God is **Satan's attack on our soul!** Amen!

References

Blum, Edwin A. I Peter, in *The Expositor's Bible Commentary*, Volume 12. Frank E. Gaebelein, ed. Grand Rapids, Michigan: Regency Reference Library/ Zondervan Publishing House, 1981.

Compton's Learning Company. *Compton's Interactive Encyclopedia*. New York: Compton's Learning Company/Compton's New Media, Inc,. 1996.

Perrucci, Robert and Marc Pilisuk. *The Triple Revolution: Emerging Social Problems in Depth*. Boston: Little, Brown, 1971.

Powell, Colin. *My American Journey*. New York; Random House, 1995.

Appendix

The Art of Preaching

Marvin A. McMickle

In his book entitled *The Making of The Sermon*, Robert McCraken suggested that preaching ought to be done with a clear set of intentions so that one knows what is being attempted and whether or not it has been achieved. McCraken suggested that there are four things the preacher can attempt to do in a sermon, and he listed them in a particular order of importance. They are to kindle the mind, energize the will, disturb the conscience, and stir the heart. Setting out to do one of these things each time one preaches is what brings both power and freshness to one's sermons.

When you preach with a sense of intention, you are attempting to make people think about their lives or about some aspect of the faith. You are trying to motivate them to engage in some action, be it social or personal, so that their works will reflect their faith. You are trying to persuade them to abandon some behavior or course of action. In short, as with the prophets of old, you are calling upon them to repent. Finally, you are giving them all of the reasons they have to rejoice in the goodness of God. Preaching should not be so preoccupied with the first three intentions that we forget that God loves to hear us praise him and to shout "Hallelujah!" And who among us does not have countless reasons to do so?

There is another advantage to preaching with intention, and it is that the shift from one theme and intended outcome to the next works to keep our preaching fresh and interesting. The greatest risk for most preachers is predictability. We limit ourselves to a few books of the Bible, a few themes and ideas, and a few well-worn illustrations. We need to find a methodology that forces us to pursue new issues, raise new questions, examine new material. Preaching with intention will help the preacher accomplish this goal.

In kindling the mind, the preacher is bringing before the people all of the controversial and complicated issues, both biblical and societal, about which they need to make up their mind. In energizing the will, the preacher is pointing to the many and various causes and activities in which Christians should be engaged if we are to be faithful to the Lord Jesus Christ. In disturbing the conscience, the preacher is doing the hardest thing that can be attempted in these days, and that is to suggest that there are limits to human behavior. There are some things that we should not do, and should not look the other way while others do. And in stirring the heart, the preacher is empowering people to realize how good God has been in their lives and then encouraging them to shout, "Hallelujah! Thank you, Jesus!" If done in succession, the preacher will cover far more material and will be a greater blessing to those who hear the word on a regular basis.

However, it takes more than good intentions to make for an effective sermon. It also takes what Aristotle referred to as **Ethos, Pathos** and **Logos**. Aristotle, who defines public speaking as "...a good man speaking well," gives even more insight into that definition with these three terms. **Ethos** refers to the integrity of the preacher. How can we preach on topics when our own lives are a contradiction of the very points we are trying to pass on to others? **Pathos** points to the passion and enthusiasm with which the word is delivered. Preaching is an energetic action. it should not only involve our words, but our hearts, our souls, our deepest convictions. **Logos** is the substance of what we want to say in any given sermon. **Logos** is the message itself.

For Aristotle, great speakers were persons of integrity who delivered with conviction a message that they believed deserved the attention and response of their hearers. The same can be said for preaching. The God we serve, the Word we deliver, and the world we are attempting to impact deserve nothing less from us than these two things.